INTRODUCTION

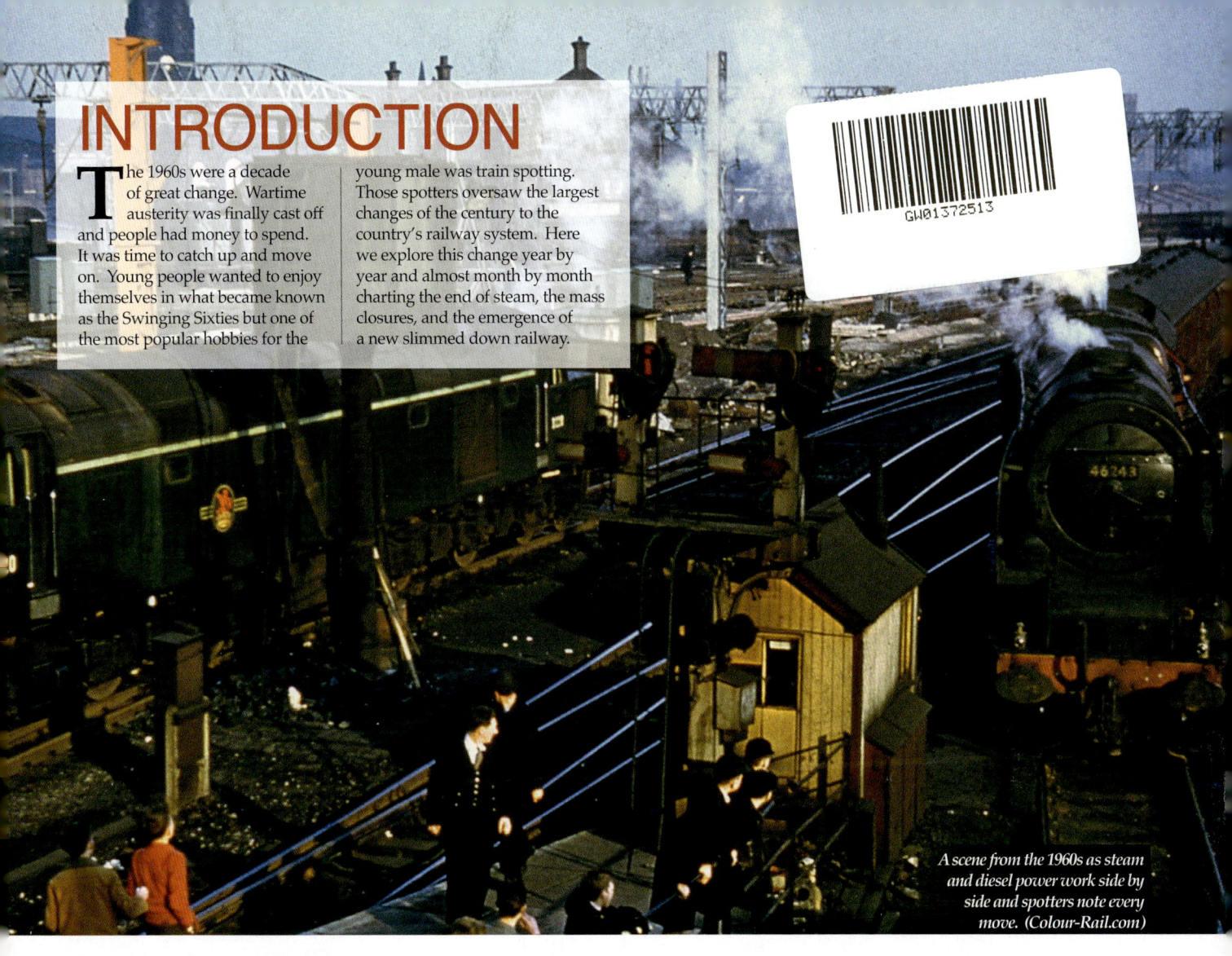

The 1960s were a decade of great change. Wartime austerity was finally cast off and people had money to spend. It was time to catch up and move on. Young people wanted to enjoy themselves in what became known as the Swinging Sixties but one of the most popular hobbies for the young male was train spotting. Those spotters oversaw the largest changes of the century to the country's railway system. Here we explore this change year by year and almost month by month charting the end of steam, the mass closures, and the emergence of a new slimmed down railway.

A scene from the 1960s as steam and diesel power work side by side and spotters note every move. (Colour-Rail.com)

CONTENTS

4	A Decade of Change	52	1966	84	Named Trains
5	The Early Years	60	1967	87	Pullmans Trains & Camping Coaches
8	1960	68	1968		
15	1961	74	1969	89	The Somerset & Dorset Joint Railway
22	1962		**1960s CAMEOS**	90	Scrap Yards
29	1963	78	Railway Safety	91	The Isle of Wight Time Capsule
37	1964	80	Evening Star	93	The Deltics
44	1965	82	Spotters, Clubs and Railtours	95	Preservation and Heritage

Editor: Paul Chancellor
Senior editor, specials: Roger Mortimer
Email: roger.mortimer@keypublishing.com
Design: Paul Ridley **Cover:** Steve Donovan

Advertising Sales Manager: Brodie Baxter
Email: brodie.baxter@keypublishing.com
Tel: 01780 755131

Advertising Production: Rebecca Antoniades
Email: rebecca.antoniades@keypublishing.com

SUBSCRIPTION/MAIL ORDER
Key Publishing Ltd, PO Box 300,
Stamford, Lincs, PE9 1NA
Tel: 01780 480404 **Fax:** 01780 757812
Subscriptions email: subs@keypublishing.com

Mail Order email: orders@keypublishing.com
Website: www.keypublishing.com/shop

PUBLISHING
Group CEO: Adrian Cox
Publisher: Mark Elliott
Chief Publishing Officer: Jonathan Jackson
Key Publishing Ltd, PO Box 100, Stamford, Lincs, PE9 1XP
Tel: 01780 755131 **Website:** www.keypublishing.com

PRINTING
Precision Colour Printing Ltd, Haldane,
Halesfield 1, Telford, Shropshire. TF7 4QQ

DISTRIBUTION
Seymour Distribution Ltd, 2 Poultry Avenue,
London, EC1A 9PU **Enquiries Line:** 02074 294000.

We are unable to guarantee the bonafides of any of our advertisers. Readers are strongly recommended to take their own precautions before parting with any information or item of value, including, but not limited to money, manuscripts, photographs or personal information in response to any advertisements within this publication.

© Key Publishing Ltd 2020
All rights reserved. No part of this magazine may be reproduced or transmitted in any form by any means, electronic or mechanical, including photocopying, recording or by any information storage and retrieval system, without prior permission in writing from the copyright owner. Multiple copying of the contents of the magazine without prior written approval is not permitted.

Many of the events described in this publication have been researched in The Railway Observer, the monthly magazine of The Railway Correspondence and Travel Society. www.RCTS.org.uk

Britain's Railways in the 1960s

INTRODUCTION

THE 1960s - A DECADE OF CULTURAL CHANGE

If the 1950s were in black and white, then the 1960s were in Technicolor. The 'Swinging Sixties' remain the defining decade of 20th century Britain. In just ten short years, London had transformed from the bleak, conservative city, only just beginning to forget the troubles of World War Two, into the capital of the world, full of freedom, hope, and promise. It was the centre of all excitement; the city where anything and everything was possible. And yet, does anyone truly know how it was possible for decades of change to take place in just ten years? Such rapid change was also reflected in our railways but before we look at that we should see the cultural context in which it all happened.

By the 1960s, the first teenage generation free from conscription emerged in Britain. Young people were finally given a voice and freedom to do what they wanted. The parents of the 1960s teenage generation had spent their youth fighting for their lives in the Second World War and wanted their own children to enjoy their youth and be able to have more fun and freedom. By the early 1960s, teenagers were already significantly different to those of a decade previously.

One of the biggest, defining aspects of the 1960s was music. It would be nice to list all the groups that gave the young people of the time so many memories, but it wasn't just the music itself - it was the access to it that also changed. The teenagers of the day had their own transistor radio, struggling to hear the fading in and out of Radio Luxembourg before the BBC finally brought them Radio 1 in 1967. With money in their pocket, and maybe a Lambretta in the garage, teenagers were able to go to the frequent live performances at the local dance hall as a multitude of groups toured the country, whilst the same music rang out in coffee bars from the juke box. That said, not all aspects of the 'Swinging Sixties' made it to the provinces. Very much like today, London was a very different place to the back to back streets of the industrial north.

The Profumo Affair, a scandalous mix of sex, spies, and government, captured the public's attention in 1963. The secretary for war John Profumo was discovered to be having an affair with a woman who was also seeing a Russian military attaché. Profumo denied the affair but later admitted that he had lied to the House of Commons and resigned.

Fashion in the decade mirrored many of the social changes. Mary Quant became famous for popularising the mini skirt which became the epitome of 1960s fashion. The mini was designed to be free and liberating and her designs used simple geometric shapes and colours which gave women a new kind of femininity. Women were free to wear more playful, youthful clothes that would have seemed outrageous ten years before. And at the end of the decade, in 1969 Neil Armstrong and Buzz Aldrin achieved the impossible by becoming the first men on the moon. It ended the decade on a note of optimism and the ability to dream for something bigger and better.

Some other events of note were
June 1960 –The BBC Television Centre opened
April 1961 - Uri Gagarin became the first man in space
November 1963 - First episode of Doctor Who was transmitted
July 1966 - England won the football World cup
January 1967 - The Forsyte Saga came to our screens
July 1967 - BBC Two provide the first full colour TV service in Europe
March 1969 - Concorde made its first supersonic test flight
■ The average house price was £2,530
■ A loaf of bread cost 1/-
■ There were 12 old pennies in one shilling and 20 shillings in the pound. One shilling=5p
■ A season ticket to see a First Division football team cost £8 10s
■ The inflation rate between the 1960s and today is approximately 2000% or 20 times ■

The changing scene - in 1960 a lady waits at Euston in clothing that had not changed in style since before the war, with battered suitcase and parcels in brown paper. Euston had not changed for many more years than the fashion. Just four years on and Euston was in the throes of demolition and the new fashions of the decade were in evidence. (Both Colour-Rail.com)

RAIL PRE 1960

BRITISH RAILWAYS- THE EARLY YEARS

To fully understand the story of our railways in the 1960s we firstly need to set the scene by looking at the preceding years and to travel back to 1923. It was in that year that the basic railway organisation structure came into being that was to remain in place well beyond the 1960s.

Prior to 1923, whilst there were several large railway companies, there were also a myriad of smaller ones. World War One (1914-18) had taken a heavy toll on the railways both financially and in respect of maintenance and infrastructure. It was decided that the more than one hundred companies would thus be amalgamated into four at what was known as the Grouping. This huge rationalisation in 1923 saw the formation of the Great Western, London Midland & Scottish, London & North Eastern and Southern Railway companies with the Great Western seeing the least change from previously as it, in the main, absorbed smaller companies into the existing organisation whereas the other three had to amalgamate large companies, as well as absorb smaller organisations, with the subsequent infighting between various factions having to be resolved before progress could be made.

In the following years various strikes and an economic depression also influenced the fortunes of the companies but that did not stop them wanting to compete. One rivalry in particular was that between the London Midland & Scottish (LMS) and London & North Eastern (LNER) for the fastest service between London and Glasgow and Edinburgh respectively, for which new locomotive designs were introduced. The LMS took the lead with the Princess Royal class, designed by William Stanier and claimed a highest speed of 114 mph before Nigel Gresley introduced the A4 Pacific for the LNER which in 1938 saw 4468 *Mallard* set a world speed record for steam of 126mph, a record which still stands.

Where the competition might have ended up, we shall never know as world events overtook the railways with the start of World War Two. During the war years, while the individual railway companies continued the railways were under government control, which was necessary to ensure the smooth movement of troops and equipment across what would have been company borders.

As in World War One, the hostilities saw railways working flat out with little time or money for much needed maintenance and government reparations failing to cover all the costs involved, so the end of the war in 1945 saw both the railway infrastructure and rolling stock in urgent need of repair and updating, but with few funds to achieve it. With a Labour government replacing the Conservatives the decision was made to nationalise the railways as from January 1st 1948 via the Transport Act of 1947, which set up British Transport Commission (BTC), of which the Railway Executive was a part and responsible for the management of the whole system, which comprised 19,639 route miles of track and operated over 20,000 steam locomotives, with 36,000 carriages and no less than 1.2 million wagons.

Relevant to the ongoing story was the next level of management, which saw the formation of six regions, with the Western & Southern being based on the former GWR and SR railways. The Scottish Region (as its name suggested) amalgamated the operations of the LMS and LNER into one north of the border. The Midland Region thus covered the old LMS territory south of the border whilst the remaining part of the former LNER was split into two, as the Eastern and North Eastern Regions, with the boundary between Doncaster and Selby. Politics soon intervened again with a Conservative government passing the Transport Act of 1953 that abolished the Railway Executive and implementing area boards under the BTC with Sir Brian Robertson as chairman.

The railways returned profits in the early years, but rapid sociological change soon saw ever mounting annual losses returned. Both freight tonnage and passenger numbers reduced as road transport developed, with transport companies being able to cherry-pick the most lucrative freight flows while car ownership was rising rapidly too. The latter possibly hit rural branch lines more than long distance services as with sparse services on the remote branches the convenience of an instantly available car far outweighed maybe a two hour wait for the next branch train. Catering for the 'holiday masses' was also often unprofitable as the season lasted only for about 12 weeks with huge Saturday peaks. Many of the extra trains provided used coaching stock that made but a single journey on ➤

The zenith of pre-war travel was the streamlined express era as witnessed on the LMS and LNER immediately before the outbreak of World War Two. Here A4 4489 Dominion of Canada *departs from Leeds in 1939. (H M Lane/Colour-rail.com)*

In the early 1950s, holiday makers crammed trains to the coast across the country. At Hopton on Sea in 1955 we see the local youngsters with their trolleys which they used to take the luggage to the hotels and boarding houses to earn a few coppers of pocket money. (Colour-Rail.com)

a Saturday and rested in a siding until required the following week, whilst spending 40 weeks going nowhere.

As the 1950s progressed another challenge faced by the railways was staff shortages as unemployment shrunk and jobs that were both clean and did not require the working of unsociable hours became plentiful. Shovelling ash out of a pit at 3am strangely became less attractive to those looking for employment.

Despite both electrification and dieselisation being widespread in the post war world, British Railways had decided to continue to build steam locomotives. For the first couple of years after nationalisation designs that had been drawn up by the big four continued to roll out of the various workshops whilst BR, under the guidance of Robert Riddles, developed what were termed the Standard designs that were to be used across the country with the first, 70000 *Britannia* appearing in 1951 with a total of 999 of various types being delivered from then until 1960.

Fast forward to 1955 and the £19m operating surplus of 1948 had become a deficit of £17m. This together with the ever increasing difficulty of getting staff to work in the dirty conditions associated with steam finally persuaded management to propose the relatively gradual replacement of steam power. Indeed, with a design life of at least 30 years it might have been reasonably expected that much of the steam power would still be in action in the mid-1980s.

A modernisation plan was drawn up for the replacement of steam engines by diesel and electric traction (the latter including parts of the East and West coast routes to Scotland) over a 15 year period at a projected cost of £1,500m. Also suggested was the replacement of many thousands of small wagons with larger ones having adequate braking, along with the provision of large new marshalling yards to reduce all the trip working between the current myriad of smaller yards, many of which were the result of the multitude of companies seen before 1923 each having their own facilities in a town or city. Track and signalling improvements also featured and the eventually agreed programme required the elimination of the BR deficit by 1962. Whilst the 1955 plan was the driver of modernisation, it should be noted that even at the time that the plan was being drawn up there were already schemes running to electrify lines in Kent and the first British Railways built

One of the earliest BR Standard designs was the 5MT 4-6-0 and the pioneer of the class 73000 is seen at Willesden when new in 1951. (C Herbert/Colour-Rail.com)

In the mid-1950s British Railways was already building DMUs at Derby Works and an early recipient of these was the Birmingham-Lichfield route. This is Four Oaks on March 10, 1956. (Colour-Rail.com)

diesel multiple units (DMUs) were under construction at Derby. With a basically proven technology it was possible to place substantial orders for more DMUs which were delivered in large numbers in the 1950s, as were approaching 1,000 diesel shunting engines of several designs with a number being based on a small number of similar machines inherited from the big four in 1948.

Mainline diesels and electrics were another matter and the 1955 edict called for a prototype evaluation plan. With the number of locomotives required, it was thought that the BR workshops would not be able to cope with the demand so a number of British manufacturers were asked to quote and build small quantities of designs in four power ranges. With the programme not being signed off until 1956, by the time that contracts had been signed, designs done and accepted and then the locomotives built it was 1958 or later before most of the prototypes appeared. Meanwhile BR's finances continued to deteriorate and in 1959 the plan was revisited. Unsurprisingly it was decided to speed up the introduction of modern traction whilst abandoning east coast electrification and pursuing the closure of uneconomic lines. It should be noted that station and line closures had been ongoing in the 1950s anyway. The unfortunate consequence of the 'speed up' decision was that large orders were placed for diesel and electric locomotives before any realistic evaluation of the prototypes had been undertaken. The result was a plethora of types, many of which had severe design flaws. Thus, the scene at the end of 1959 was that of a railway suffering falling passenger numbers and freight tonnage, which unsurprisingly resulted in ever larger deficits. Most of the ravages of the war had been repaired but the infrastructure, both in terms of routes and structures, was much as it had been back in 1923. Some express passenger services were by this time being diesel locomotive hauled and an army of diesel shunters had displaced a lot of local yard steam duties.

The widespread deployment of DMUs had improved the lot for many commuters and branch lines where the new traction was employed even saw passenger numbers rise, however as we shall see, not by enough in many cases to make lines profitable.

In the following pages we shall look at the events and changes year by year through the 1960s and then explore some of the subjects in more detail. ■

Among the earliest of the locomotives to arrive because of the Modernisation plan were the North British built Warship Type 4s. Keen to show off the new engines they were allocated to front line duties such as The Royal Duchy, seen here at Exeter on Jul 22, 1958 worked by D600 Active. (Colour-Rail.com)

Britain's Railways in the 1960s

7

1960
OVERVIEW

At the dawn of the decade few would have predicted the vast changes that would occur in the coming ten years, either in society or more specifically on our railways. Wartime austerity and its legacy had finally passed, and the country was entering a time of growth and improving living standards, one major effect being that rapidly increasing numbers of people had access to a means of personal motorised transport. The Conservative government appeared to be pro road transport and was investing heavily in new and improved roads whilst wishing to eliminate payments to support nationalised industries, of which the railways were at the forefront in respect of losses.

At a practical level British Railways opened the year with 14,457 steam engines, 1,799 diesel, and 85 electric locomotives on its books, as well as 54 steam and diesel types in its departmental stock. There was also one gas turbine - the Western Region Brown-Boveri 18000. In addition, it operated 1,911 DMU cars, 2,000 electric, 22 railbuses and one battery railcar.

Illustrating the speed at which large organisations moved, or rather didn't, the Scottish Region introduced a divisional organisation in May, it being the last region to do this despite the fact that it had been recommended in the 1954 White Paper.

Regrettably, hooliganism was no less of a problem sixty years ago than it is today with an anticipated cost of £500,000 for the full year. Excursion, late night, and weekend trains saw the most damage to rolling stock, with 250 cases in four months being recorded on the North Eastern Region and 1,000 cases on the LMR in the London area. To try and improve the traveller's lot, litter bins were fitted to Clacton line coaches, but all had been ripped out within a week. The report for the year made no mention of two modern day problems, cable theft and graffiti.

The year before the decade began, 1959 had seen in the introduction of four-character headcodes - the train reporting number system - which was to replace the different systems inherited at nationalisation. These had not been widely adopted in 1959 but 1960 saw the full introduction across all regions except the Southern which used them for interregional services but not for internal duties.

The close of the year saw the publication of a White Paper which proposed the abolition of the British Transport Commission and its replacement by four boards having responsibility for the railways, London Transport, canals, and docks. Catering and road haulage were to be put into new independent companies. Each group would have full commercial independence and, on the railways, the £1,600m of outstanding debt would see £400m written off, with the balance made subject to 'special arrangements'. A return to profitability was targeted for 1965.

Modern Traction scene
The planned schedule for new locomotive deliveries in the year totalled 947 of no less than 25 different classes - standardisation it was not. Services due for the introduction of diesel multiple units during the year were many and varied. They included Manchester Central to Liverpool Central, Marylebone to Aylesbury and High Wycombe, Manchester and Rochdale to Wigan and Southport, Bolton to Wigan and Hull to Leeds and thence to Liverpool. Additionally there were York to Wakefield and Manchester, Bradford and Burnley to Blackpool, Aberdeen to Inverness, Winchester to Reading, and London to East Grinstead and Tunbridge Wells. In the southwest there was Taunton to Penzance along with the Kingswear and Falmouth branches, while in the northwest there were Wellington (Salop) to Chester, Shrewsbury to Aberystwyth and other Cambrian routes plus the Central Wales line and Whitchurch to Welshpool. Electrification schemes expected to go live were various routes from Liverpool Street, Manchester to Crewe and the Glasgow suburban network. Overall, more than 50% of all passenger miles were to be worked by diesel and electric multiple units.

However, the stock of front line diesel power was minimal whilst nearly all the large passenger steam classes remained substantially intact.

The former LMS lines had received just nine Derby-built

The GWR inspired experiment with gas turbine power was winding down with the surviving loco 18000 spending much time languishing at Swindon works as seen here. (T Owen/Colour-Rail.com)

Six months after delivery Metro Cammell DMU E51546 stands at Neville Hill shed and on occasions would work the Manchester-York route. (G H Hunt/Colour-Rail.com)

1960

Sulzer type 4 engines, D1-D9 and also D205-D236 of the English Electric (EE) Type 4s giving them a total of 41 express passenger locomotives, all of which were employed on West Coast mainline duties from Euston.

On former LNER routes, they had received the very first EE Type 4s D200-D204 in 1958 and those five machines were put to work on some of the Liverpool Street to Norwich duties previously the domain of the Britannia Pacifics, but with only five engines and initial poor availability, they had yet to make much of an impact. In the process of delivery were further members of the class starting at D237 and 16 of these had just begun to oust steam from the East Coast mainline out of Kings Cross.

Over on the Western Region the two pilot batches of Warship diesel hydraulics, the North British built D600-D604 and Swindon built D800-2 had been in service for two years in some cases and had already led to the decision to mass produce the Swindon design at the expense of that from North British and D803-D814 had been delivered. These 20 machines had already had an impact being used on services from Paddington to Bristol and the West Country appearing on prestige services such as the Cornish Riviera Express and the Bristolian.

Life on the Southern was less dramatic. No front line express diesel types were in service or planned, the way forward seen as a gradual expansion of the electrification programme utilising electric multiple units. Indeed, the region had the most modern fleet of express steam power with the 140 Bulleid Pacifics being youngsters at 20 years or less. Nonetheless, in the electrified area of Kent it was envisaged that key passenger services such as the Golden Arrow and the Night Ferry would remain loco-hauled, and for this work and some freight duties, third rail electric engines were in the course of delivery with E5001-13 already in stock.

There were far greater numbers of the lower powered diesels active at the start of the decade from a multiplicity of classes. The largest class at the time was the Brush 1,365hp Type 2, where deliveries had totalled 77 by the end of 1959 (D5500-76), with all of them employed on the Eastern Region. Suburban services out of Kings Cross had also been handled by ten English Electric Type 2s, D5900-9 which later became known as the Baby Deltics, and the North British built D6100-37. Both these designs were to attract notoriety in years to come for their poor reliability. Showing just how the failure to wait until evaluation of prototypes had been completed before placing bulk orders was the fact that the Eastern had to work with even a ➤

English Electric Type 4s entered service on the East Coast mainline in quantity in 1960 and D276 heads south at Hadley Wood. (Colour-Rail.com)

Britain's Railways in the 1960s

Soon to be banished to Cumbria, Metrovick D5711 lived in a steam age environment when stabled at Bedford on January 10, 1960. (Colour-Rail.com)

fourth variety of the Type 2, this being the 1,160hp Sulzer engined type from BRCW, of which 47 had been delivered in 1958/9. D5300-19 went to London area sheds but D5320 onwards went to Scotland, all initially based at Edinburgh. Performing similar duties on the Midland was the Derby Works built equivalent where D5000-48/50-60 were in service as were the Metrovick Co-Bo s D5700-19, another design that was proved wanting.

That said, 15 of the D5000s were in fact on loan to the Southern Region pending delivery of new engines in 1960. The only Type 2 to have reached the Western Region was the hydraulic version of the North British design with just D6300-4/6 in service.

The Midland and Eastern also had Type 1 power (1,000hp or less) in the shape of English Electric D8000-30 for the former and BTH built D8200-17 and North British D8400-9 for the latter. The most powerful engines in service were the 2,200hp Warships from D803 upwards and the Peaks D1-D10 (2,300hp), with all the other Type 4s being of 2,000hp. It should be noted that there were no examples of a Type 3 (1,750hp) on the system at all, and yet that size of engine was seen to be the equivalent of a Class 5 steam engine of which the likes of the Western Halls, Midland Stanier 5MTs and the Eastern B1s were seen as the backbone of everyday operations. Mention should also be made of the first electric locomotives delivered for the Euston to Crewe and Liverpool electrification scheme, although no trains ran with electric power on the route at the start of the 1960s.

The new year started with the arrival of more newly constructed diesel and electric locomotives with deliveries of various types taking place nearly every month for much of the decade. Noteworthy in January however was the first Type 3 to arrive built by BRCW as D6500 for the Southern Region. It was planned that the Southern would not use steam heated rolling stock, unlike all other areas of the country, and so the D6500s were the first mainline engines not to be fitted with steam heating boilers, an item of equipment that proved to be problematic for years to come. Unfortunately, the required electrically heated coaching stock was not yet available on the Southern, so the new diesels could not operate passenger services until well into the spring, with the aforementioned D5000s

The first D6500 locos were received on the Southern Region and D6502 is seen at Bromley in June 1960. It proved to be a rare picture of this engine which was soon involved in an accident and withdrawn. (Colour-Rail.com)

1960

The North British Type 2s were all moved to Scotland during the year. However, doing a good job keeping out of the public eye was D6129 at Mellis in Suffolk in May. (Colour-Rail.com)

being retained for that work in the southeast corner of the region.

A small exhibition of new motive power was held at Marylebone on April 27 and 28, 1960 featuring D269, D5081, E3037, E5012 together with two EMU coaches and one DMU vehicle. A point to be highlighted, as it comes to the fore frequently in the early years of the decade, was the autonomy of each of the regions. This manifested itself, especially on the Western, with its policy of diesel hydraulic power when all other orders for mainline diesels were diesel electrics.

February saw the Scottish Region receive the first of a second batch of North British type 2s with the arrival of D6138 which went new to Aberdeen. Indeed, the scene in Scotland, particularly the north, was to change quite rapidly in 1960. To bring some standardisation to the Eastern Region diesel fleet, D5300-19 and D6100-37 were all moved north of the border during the year. The move of the unsuccessful North British machines was reportedly to have them near to their Glasgow based builders, whilst cynics opined that they were being hidden as far from headquarters as possible.

New electric multiple units under construction in the year included 4-EPB sets for the Southern Region, primarily intended to replace existing electric stock, and units for East Anglia where the last of 112 for Tilbury services had been completed with work then starting on units for Enfield line duties. York Carriage & Wagon Works was responsible for the construction.

A new introduction on the system was the 'Mini Buffet' which were intended to be used in place of Restaurant Cars where demand was low, with the first of the type being displayed at Glasgow Buchannan Street at the end of March.

On the Great Eastern section, the final phases of the suburban electrification scheme started operation running to Chingford, Hertford East, and Bishops Stortford, whilst diesel units worked to Cheshunt via the Lea Valley. However, as seems to be just as much the case 60 years later, the new stock had many technical issues and initial services did not run as planned and sets were borrowed from the Southend line with some journeys covered by diesel units. Such was the scale of the problem that 71 new units of two classes were withdrawn for modification after just a few weeks and service frequencies were reduced as not enough additional stock could be drafted in. What were billed as the last steam-hauled suburban trains from Liverpool Street ran on November 20. The Glasgow Blue Train electrics had also commenced operation, but trouble also loomed there with an explosion on one of the EMUs on December 13 with injuries to some passengers and the guard. A second explosion occurred on December 17 with the use of the electric units stopped immediately afterwards. Unlike the Liverpool Street scheme where other electric units were available, the Scottish Region had to revert back to steam haulage and a major operation took place on Sunday, December 18 to recover all the old coaching stock and steam locomotives that had been used previously to restart the service the following day.

December saw the demise of one item of Modern Traction motive power when the second of the gas turbine engines ordered by the GWR, 18000 was condemned leaving just prototype GT3 to try and promote the gas turbine cause.

Steam Happenings

The start-of-year total of steam engines was a reduction of over 25% from the figure at the time of nationalisation, this being achieved partly by a number of branch closures, but in the main the large scale introduction of DMUs on branch and commuter services and diesel shunters for freight yard duties.

Despite the influx of diesels, steam power was not to be outdone in January when the penultimate delivery of steam engines entered service in the shape of a pair of 9F 2-10-0s 92218 and 92219. They'd ➤

During their brief period of operation in 1960, a Glasgow Blue Train stands at Balloch on November 7. (Colour-Rail.com)

Britain's Railways in the 1960s

been built at Swindon and were sent to work in South Wales, yet at the same time Swindon works was also condemning tank engine types, some of which had only been built in the previous six or seven years, this despite the fact that elsewhere in the country steam engines built in the previous century were still very much at work on the network. The withdrawal for scrap of six year old engines made little apparent sense when in the North Eastern Region engines built in 1909 were still receiving overhauls to work duties that the western types could have handled with ease. Examples of 'joined up thinking' appeared to be rare with the only one to stand out being the transfer of two 16XX 0-6-0PTs to Scotland in the late 1950s to replace aging power on the Dornoch branch.

Returning to the steam scene, an ongoing programme of rebuilding a number of Bullied Pacifics of the West Country and Battle of Britain classes was still underway on the Southern, whilst engines such as Castles continued to be upgraded by the fitting of a double chimney. Even steam engine namings were continuing with several Southern Region BR Standard 5MTs receiving names previously carried by now withdrawn King Arthur class engines. However, a sign of things to come was the withdrawal of LNER A2/2 60501 *Cock 'o the North*. March saw one of the most significant events of railway history when British Railways put its last built steam locomotive into traffic when 92220 *Evening Star* left Swindon works after naming, in full lined green livery with a GWR style copper capped chimney. We will look at the history of this locomotive in more detail later. It was not of course the last steam locomotive to be built as production of industrial tank engines continued for a number of years and few would have predicted the appearance of new build steam engines such as A1 replica *Tornado* in the next century. Followers of all things Great Western may have been worried by the condemnation of one of the first Castle class 5005 *Manorbier Castle* in March, following as it did that of Hall 5915 the previous month. September saw the withdrawal of the last steam engine in service that had been built for the North London Railway, 0-6-0 tank 58850. However, it did not suffer the fate of the scrap yard being acquired for use on the nascent Bluebell Railway. Former Great Central railway designs also came out of service such as the final member of the first batch of Director 4-4-0s 62666 *Zeebrugge* as well as the last 2-6-4 tank this being A5 class 69820.

The Eastern Region saw some substantial service and motive power changes towards the year

0-6-0PT 1646 is waiting to enter Skelbo on March 3, 1960, a long way from its Swindon birthplace. (Colour-Rail.com)

The year saw the final D11/1 4-4-0 62666 Zeebrugge condemned. In a scene that was to become very familiar in the years to come the engine awaits its fate at Doncaster on December 14. (Colour-Rail.com)

end. The express service from Grimsby to Kings Cross had long been operated by B1 4-6-0s whereas most of the other long distance services had Pacific power. With diesels spreading rapidly in East Anglia some of the Britannia Pacifics used on the expresses to Norwich from Liverpool Street became surplus and a small batch were transferred to Immingham to work the Grimsby services.

Infrastructure and Rolling Stock

The gradual run down of the system continued with for instance, St Albans and Bournville sheds being closed. But work was underway at Newton Abbot preparing the old steam depot to be a diesel shed, whilst it was announced that Bath Road depot in Bristol would be closed at the end of the summer timetable to be demolished to make way for a completely new diesel facility. Similar plans were announced for the shed site at Swansea Landore.

Something else that has gone full circle in recent years is the Bletchley flyover. This was under construction in 1960 to improve traffic flow on the West Coast mainline by removing the conflicting movements of trains on the Oxford to Cambridge route, which needed to cross the mainline here. Subsequently the route was closed but is now very much on the reopening agenda bringing new life to the structure. The West Coast route was of course in the process of being electrified at this time. To facilitate this, services had been either slowed down or thinned which particularly affected the services to Birmingham, where passengers were encouraged to travel via the former Great Western route. At the same time, the M1 was under construction and bus and coach operator Midland Red applied to run five express services daily via that route.

Some improvements, whilst vital to the fortunes of the railway, were not always evident to the average traveller. One such might have been a £2.75m plan to modernise signalling in the Reading area covering the route from Twyford through to Cholsey, Midgham and Bramley with associated track works, such as relaying 20mph limited crossovers with those that could be used at 40mph. Work was also underway at Newport (South Wales) on a major signalling scheme, again with associated track layout improvements. Announcements were made about the construction of vast marshalling yards at Gloucester and Shrewsbury, schemes that never came to pass.

Services

Pressure to reduce losses meant that the provision of services was constantly under review, and not just for branch lines, as evidenced by a meeting of the Transport Users

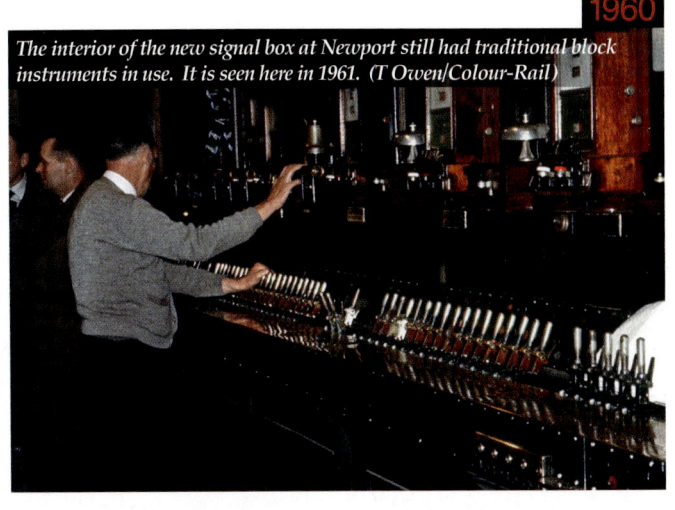

The interior of the new signal box at Newport still had traditional block instruments in use. It is seen here in 1961. (T Owen/Colour-Rail)

Consultative Council (TUCC) at Carlisle which had been asked to consider the closure of the line from Barnard Castle to Penrith. On that occasion it declined to decide, instead recommending that an 18 month stay of execution be granted. Another line that BR had in its sights for closure was the Hope Valley route through Edale, one that did escape the axe, but if you wanted to travel to Kilsby & Crick between Rugby and Northampton you would have been too late as it closed on February 1.

Station and route closures continued throughout the year with for instance in November, passenger services being withdrawn between Aintree Central and Gatacre with five stations closing and another service to go was that between Macclesfield Hibel Road and Uttoxeter via Leek. The uneconomic state of some services can be seen when looking at that from Burton on Trent on the 5.5 mile journey to Tutbury which was said to be used by an average of 12 passengers per day. No hope situations such as that were however balanced by the opening of Park Leaze Halt which was on the Cirencester branch. This was part of efforts to build passenger numbers following the introduction of railbuses on that and the Tetbury branch in 1959. Some 2,500 passengers per week were said to be using the Cirencester route but only 12,800 passengers in the year booked from Tetbury, nonetheless this was 2.5 times greater than had been using the steam service.

Another service improvement from April 25 was that on the Redditch branch. This station was on the route from Birmingham New Street to Ashchurch which had an infrequent steam worked through service. However, Redditch was being developed as a New Town and had been served by nine trains daily, but the new diesel-worked service provided 19 trains between there and New Street.

Observations

While diesel power was becoming much more prevalent on the prestige services on both the Western and Midland Regions, on the East Coast route, despite the arrival of a quantity of English Electric Type 4s, the front line expresses such as the Flying Scotsman were still steam worked, usually by an A4 Pacific. A typical example of their work was that ➤

A diesel railbus approaches one of the newest stations on the network, this being Park Leaze Halt which opened in 1960. It also had one of the shortest lives, closing again in 1964. (T Owen/Colour-Rail.com)

1960

of 60022 *Mallard* in w/c April 2 when it worked the down Flying Scotsman every day as far as Newcastle, returning from there on the 5pm service to London, amassing over 3,200 miles in the week. The East Coast Pacifics were set to maintain their pre-eminent position until the arrival of the 3,300hp Deltic diesels, 22 of which were on order for the route. That said, diagrams employing three EE Type 4s between Newcastle and Kings Cross commenced on May 2. However, the non-stop Elizabethan running between Edinburgh and London, was scheduled to remain steam-hauled throughout the season and it transpired that only six locomotives were used for the 90 day duration of the train, these being 60012/24/5/7/9/32.

April saw the start of a three hour timing for several trains between Edinburgh and Aberdeen using pairs of BRCW diesels, although this was little faster than pre-war steam schedules. Diesel units also took over numerous services around Fife. A line that has become a favourite with enthusiasts was the Somerset & Dorset route from Bath Green Park to Bournemouth West and we will look at this in more detail later. It was a difficult line to operate due to its steep gradients and always required double heading to be employed on the holiday trains from the north and Midlands to the south coast. Thus, trials with a single 9F, 92204, on the line at the end of March were significant. These proved successful and Bath shed received a summer allocation of the class for the first time later in the year.

Despite nationalisation having taken place 12 years earlier, many relics of the past lived on including some locomotive liveries, with two 0-6-0 pannier tanks employed on Paddington empty stock duties still carrying GWR livery. In a 'blast from the past' the North Eastern Region even re-introduced the old LNER Apple green on two J72 class tank engines employed on station pilot duties at York and Newcastle.

One of the big draws to the hobby of train spotting was the fact that along with the mundane and everyday workings of engines there was always the chance of something rare turning up. With only ten engines in the class, the BR Standard Clan Pacifics could never be called common, although they were seen daily in northwest England and southern Scotland. Thus, the appearance of 72005 *Clan MacGregor* at Bristol on July 9 would really have been a noteworthy event. Just how many spotters saw it is a moot point as it arrived in the city at a reported 3.15am on a train from Bradford and left again before noon the following day. ∎

The Elizabethan heads through Burnmouth in August headed by 60025 Falcon, one of just six A4s used on the train during the season.

J72 68723, resplendent in Apple green, performs station pilot duties at Newcastle in 1960 alongside a Metro Cammell DMU carrying the 'cats whiskers' livery of the time. (Colour-Rail.com)

14   Britain's Railways in the 1960s

1961 OVERVIEW

Leeds City was typical of large stations around the country, looking much as it had 50 years previously and begrimed with dirt. Rebuilding work had ground to a halt. D49s 62700/53 add another layer of soot as they await departure. (L W Rowe/Colour-Rail.com)

More than 950 diesel and electric locomotives should have been delivered during 1960 but only 801 arrived, giving an opening stock of 2,635 and, of the 801, only around 100 were intended for express passenger duties. DMU and EMU stock deliveries (individual carriages, not units) totalled 584 of which 205 were electrics. When justifying the purchase of modern traction, it was always the case that 'x number of diesels could do the work of y number of steam engines'. Taking a very moderate ratio of 3:2 and estimating that 584 DMU/EMU carriages equated to some 180 units, it might have been expected that a total of 981 new locos and units would have replaced around 1,460 steam engines, but only 1,181 were withdrawn and that takes no account of the various line closures that should have seen an even greater number laid aside. Thus, a combination of poor reliability and lack of efficiency in deploying the new power helped lead to the continued worsening of the financial position during 1961.

An event that might have passed many enthusiasts by, and certainly few of whom appreciated the long term significance, was the appointment of Dr Richard Beeching to head the industry, his only connection to the railways being that he commuted by train each day, his previous role being as a director of Imperial Chemical Industries. His brief was to return the industry to profitability. With the retirement of a couple of senior managers on December 31 a major shakeup of those remaining took place ready for the start of 1962. An example of the changing mind set of BR was seen in respect of the rebuilding of Leeds City station where work had been stopped to save money. In response to a question from a local MP, Dr Beeching suggested that the local authority should consider contributing to the cost of the work, which was not well received locally.

Traditionally timetable books were produced by each region covering all its services and those that worked to and from other regions into its area. However, BR announced in 1961 that they intended to produce a national timetable in 1962 covering all long distance and important connecting services. Another development saw some regions produce timetable booklets to promote new local diesel services.

It is difficult to give an overview of traction use across the country at the end of 1961. Suffice to say that many local and branch services were in the hands of units whilst diesel locomotives were handling most of the timetabled expresses emanating from the capital except on the Southern Region and on the Western to South Wales and Wolverhampton, whilst much freight traffic remained steam-hauled.

That said, areas such as Kent, East Anglia, the far southwest of England along with the north of Scotland were rapidly becoming no go areas for steam. Conversely, other than on the mainline, steam reigned supreme in much of northwest England and Wales.

Modern Traction Scene

The EE Type 4s on the Midland Region finally made their mark by working the high profile named trains such as the Royal Scot and The Caledonian. But compared to the 8P rating of the Duchesses, which they replaced, they were woefully under powered for the job. The first of the production Deltics to arrive at Doncaster for testing was D9001 on February 23 with D9000 arriving on February 28 and they worked acceptance trials of 14 coaches between Grantham and Peterborough. March 7 saw D9001 on the very first Deltic passenger duty on the East Coast route. D9000/2 were used by Haymarket and Gateshead sheds respectively for crew training during March and April.

May 16 saw the official handover of the first Hymek Type 3, D7000 built by Beyer Peacock of which eventually 101 would be produced. These would take over many of the less arduous duties on the Western Region replacing the likes of Halls and Granges - at least that was the plan. An order was placed for yet another new diesel locomotive type, this being a 275hp 0-6-0 design specifically for shunting ➤

Steam still reigned supreme on services to Paddington from South Wales, Worcester, and the Midlands. 6021 King Richard II was heading for the capital when photographed at Leamington in November. (G Parry Collection/Colour-Rail.com)

Britain's Railways in the 1960s

Celebrating just one week in service, an almost new D102 heads north through Ambergate on May 27, 1961. (Colour-Rail.com)

duties in Southampton docks to replace the incumbent USA tanks.

The continuing delivery of the Peak class, the production series being uprated to 2,500hp from the first batch at 2,300hp, saw many services on the old Midland Railway route out of St Pancras succumb to diesel power. Some of the class were also by now going to the North Eastern Region at Leeds and one was at Bristol for driver training, so it would not be long before the replacement of steam power on both the Settle and Carlisle route and Newcastle to Bristol would commence.

With very few Type 4 and no Type 3 engines allocated to Scottish depots, internal services were operated by Type 2s, both singly and in pairs, but all was not well, with the D5300s used on Edinburgh–Aberdeen trains suffering from fires, whilst the D6100s continued to give grief generally with the latest ailment, a burnt out generator, being reported on six locomotives in a two month period.

An experiment that slipped through almost unnoticed, of something which today we take for granted, was the fitting of disc brakes on Southern EMU 4CEP 7102 in November.

An arrival of note was the delivery in December of Western D1000 *Western Enterprise*. Painted in Desert Sand livery it certainly made an impression, but the colour would not really have been practical in everyday use.

It was one of 630 diesel locomotives that arrived in the year which comprised Peaks D20-D49 and D85-D148, EE Type 4s D315-D371, Warships D830-2, D840/3-58 and D866-70 all of which were 2,000hp or above. Type 3 arrivals were D6538-82, D6701-34, and D7000-15 whilst Types 1 and 2 continued to arrive in quantity including no fewer than 60 English Electric Type 1s D8050-D8109. Despite the contraction of freight duties there were also 187 shunters delivered. Not to be omitted were 20 of the 22 Deltics and 23 electric locos for the West Coast completed the locomotive fleet. The DMU fleet saw just 116 carriages added whilst electric stock increased by 160.

Steam Happenings

The Bulleid Pacific rebuilding programme continued in 1961 with 34024/98 being released from Eastleigh works in February. That left 34096/7 and 34108-9 remaining to be dealt with to complete the programme which meant that 50 engines would stay in original condition. The double chimney programme for Castles and Southern based Standard 4MTs also continued.

Veteran power continued to be employed in Scotland, but at much

D1000 Western Enterprise showed off its impractical livery of Desert Sand outside Swindon works shortly after completion. (Colour-Rail.com)

Britain's Railways in the 1960s

reduced levels with the former Caledonian and LMS 2P types being particularly under threat, but the equally old ex-LNER 0-6-0s continued to thrive on coal traffic in Eastern Scotland. Steam in the north of Scotland was by now being replaced with the use of DMUs on Aberdeen to Inverness workings, with few steam trains existing north of Inverness.

Whilst, as noted above, the production Deltics had started to arrive, and indeed were rostered to work the Flying Scotsman and Talisman, there were not enough of them in service to take on the nonstop Elizabethan and so against all the odds the ultimate steam duty was again covered by the A4 Pacifics for the duration with 60028/31 working the first services. On the final day, September 9, 60009/22 were employed, interestingly both surviving into preservation, with eight different class members being used in total.

One feature of the early 1960s was the number of locations where engines were held in store although they were not withdrawn. These tended to be redundant goods yards or branches rather than the normal shed locations and lists of stored engines were circulated by some railway societies. With the large number of engines being withdrawn another development was the scrapping of locomotives by contractors. Until the late 1950s it was traditional that all engines were cut up by the British Railways works but throughout the 1960s withdrawn engines were sold off and moved, sometimes a considerable distance, to be delivered to private scrapyards with sites spread around the UK. Although many were in areas where there were also steel works to minimise the distance that the scrap had to be moved for reprocessing.

Another rare example of joined up thinking became evident with the transfer of the whole of the fleet of Western Region Britannias to the Midland Region at the end of the summer timetable. With Kings available and several Castles being transferred in to replace the Britannias, Cardiff had enough express power to manage without the 7MTs. As some were allocated to Carlisle and rapidly appeared on duties to Perth there will have been some very surprised number takers in that area. At the same time, the rule of the Britannias in East Anglia came to an end with all express work being rostered for diesel traction thereafter.

The effects of the diesel invasion were finally felt on the steam fleet although not in a pattern that might be expected. The LMR withdrew six of the Princess Royal class along with three Jubilees and nine Patriots while the Eastern removed three A2s and six A3s from its front line passenger power. Despite having received many Warships the Western accounted for just three Castles and eight Halls and it was left to the Southern Region to really attack its passenger fleet with six Lord Nelsons, 14 King Arthurs and 15 Schools heading for the scrap line. It was indeed many of the smaller engines that fell by the wayside in the year, with several classes becoming extinct. No fewer than 770 0-6-0 tender and tank engines were on the condemnation list.

Infrastructure and Rolling Stock

Despite a constant stream of new carriages entering traffic, some pre grouping stock remained in everyday service. On Culm Valley services two coaches built by the Barry Railway remained active ➤

Battle of Britain 34109 Sir Trafford Leigh-Mallory was one of the last of the class to be rebuilt. Seen here at Hook it is just weeks away from its call to works for conversion. (T Owen/Colour-Rail.com)

The use of Britannia Pacifics from Liverpool Street to Norwich came to an end in 1961. Here 70007 Coeur de Lion awaits departure from the capital in March. In due course it would become the first of the class to be condemned when resident at Carlisle Kingmoor. (Colour-Rail.com)

Britain's Railways in the 1960s

The rural backwater of the Hemyock branch in Devon was served by an ex Barry Railway carriage for many years, often accompanied by milk tankers. Here 1470 is seen at the terminus with the branch train in 1961. (Colour-Rail.com)

whilst all the stock used on the Isle of Wight was also of pre-1923 vintage.

The London, Tilbury and Southend (LTS) electrification and resignalling scheme saw a new signal box opened at Upminster in February, along with overhead line testing between Shoeburyness and Leigh, although electric services were not expected to run until September, with a revised timetable not coming into force until 1962, but initial trial running started on June 25, 1961.

Work on a new marshalling yard at Carlisle Kingmoor continued through the year whilst a £9m scheme to build a new yard and diesel depot at Tinsley was announced. It was planned to close nine existing marshalling yards and five engine sheds when the scheme was complete, this not being due until the end of 1964. Typical of the more mundane conversions for diesel power was that at Holbeck, where the old works and some roads of the steam shed were being rebuilt for the new occupants. A completely new depot was planned for Margam, again in association with a new marshalling yard, whilst a further stage of the Newport resignalling was completed.

Another announcement concerned the building of new engineering facilities at Derby at a cost of £1m which were to be used for research including carriage and wagon under frames, bridge sections and reinforced concrete items.

The maintenance of the Severn Tunnel posed many problems, one of which was to repair the concrete mushroom which formed a cover over a plug in the strata. The structure measured some 15ft wide and 3ft high and was on an outcrop of rock ¼ mile from the shore. With the vast rise and fall of the tide here the working window was only some three hours and required the workers to row to the rock along with the required cement and tools each time and then wheel barrow the supplies to the mushroom. Even small repairs were taking ten men two to three weeks to carry out. On June 15, a helicopter was used for the first time to carry ready

The overhead wires are up but steam still reigns at Shoeburyness on April 20, 1961. Full electric services would not start until 1962. (K Fairey/Colour-Rail.com)

1961

The end was nigh for the Upton on Severn branch which closed in August. Pannier 7788 was seen at the station in March. (R Denison/Colour-Rail.com)

mixed concrete directly to the site vastly reducing the duration of the repair work.

Another innovation was the installation of closed circuit television at Paddington to 'speed up communication' between the various departments.

Work continued throughout the period on the West Coast electrification scheme with a new signal box completed at Coventry in the autumn. Meanwhile the first section to be finished was that from Liverpool to Crewe, with the intention of starting limited use of electric power from January 1, 1962.

Whilst most infrastructure items were positive, one that was not was the demolition of an arch of the Severn rail bridge when a barge collided with it, thus severing the route from Berkeley Road through to South Wales. The span was not replaced and thus the route was closed.

Services
Trans Pennine services had seen the introduction of six-car diesel multiple units from January 2 along with a revision of the timetable due to their superior power/weight ratio. A large upturn in coal traffic was noted in the Blyth area of Northumberland with most trains being worked by the then ageing J27 0-6-0s, several of which had already been withdrawn. It was decided that the remaining class members would be retained to handle the increased traffic and as we shall see they eventually outlived many hundreds of their younger brethren.

Station closures continued with Dewsbury (Market Place) being an early casualty. Also targeted for closure was the line from Keighley to Oxenhope where the TUCC carried out an 'evaluation visit' on February 20. Other lines under threat early in 1961 were Taunton-Barnstaple and Ashchurch to Upton upon Severn, the latter receiving swift execution with closure on August 12.

A major closure proposal was for the withdrawal of the Eastern and Western valley services emanating from Newport which had only relatively recently been switched to diesel operation. It removed the likes of Blaenavon, Brynmawr and Ebbw Vale from the passenger map.

September 11 was a black day for stations in Lincolnshire and on the March to Doncaster line with no fewer than 29 being closed.

The North Eastern TUCC which had looked at the viability of the Barnard Castle-Penrith route in 1960 recommended on March 21 that it should remain open 'indefinitely' and yet on June 8 they voted for closure as the North Western TUCC, which was responsible for part of the line, refused to back the original decision.

Timetable changes announced for the summer service in general saw just minor amendments from what went before, but one notable achievement was the acceleration of the down Aberdonian, which had 54 minutes taken out of its Kings-Cross-Edinburgh timings. Another line to see improvements was that from Norwich to London where 16 EE Type 3s were to be deployed, but initially not all were available and even those that were also deputising for unavailable Type 2s and 4s. While most service accelerations were associated with the introduction of diesel power, the Southern timetable for Winter 1961 saw the speeding up of the steam-worked Atlantic Coast Express with seven minutes being removed from the down train schedule and eleven minutes shaved from the up service requiring average speeds in excess of 60mph.

The Southern Region had limited opportunities for high speed running but on the Eastern the new timetable included 29 runs in excess of an average 60mph with The West Riding becoming the fastest train in the country by running from ➤

The Atlantic Coast Express was speeded up in 1961. Merchant Navy 35003 Royal Mail heads the train at Sidmouth Junction on this occasion. (Colour-Rail.com)

Britain's Railways in the 1960s   19

Hitchin to Retford at an average speed of 71.8 mph.

By September nearly all commuter services from Marylebone had been taken over by DMUs running in four and eight car formations, leaving just a much reduced service of longer distance trains in the hands of steam engines. Paddington was another station where most of the commuter services along the Thames Valley were now in the hands of DMUs. Yet another steam deletion came on the Southern Region where no services from the capital to the old SECR lines now had steam power.

It has been a challenge to uncover information about some of the workings that just faded away as the years went by such as excursion traffic. Rambler's excursions were becoming rarer by 1961 but when they did run, they were popular with an eight-coach DMU conveying 550 people from Bradford and Leeds which took the walkers to Coxwold, Helmsley, Nawton and Kirkbymoorside on April 16. The under-threat Hope Valley line saw no less than seven special trains arrive on June 11 to celebrate Rambler's Week from as far afield as Nottingham and Liverpool.

Boat train services to the Channel Islands used to run from both Southampton and Weymouth under the auspices of the Southern and Great Western Railways respectively. The Southern Region gained control of Weymouth in 1958 and consolidated all Channel Islands boat services there from 1961.

Despite investing in buffet facilities for several DMUs in Scotland, those that had been provided on services from Glasgow to Stranraer were closed from the start of the summer timetable, although the carriages remained in each train.

Lord Nelson 30864 Sir Martin Frobisher approaches Southampton with a Bournemouth to Birkenhead train, a through journey that would no longer be possible from the start of the winter timetable. (L W Rowe/Colour-Rail.com)

The number of car carrying services gradually grew in the decade and whilst some were weekend-only trains with cars carried on flatbed wagons, others ran almost daily and to increase car carrying capacity 14 double-deck covered vehicles were ordered for use on the Kings-Cross to Edinburgh service, these being the first of their kind in the country. The roof and side panels of each were made from fibre glass. The service had been introduced in 1955 carrying 50,000 cars in the first six years.

Despite the BR designed Mk1 carriage having been in production for much of the 1950s, and most express services being formed with them, ordering and delivery of catering vehicles had not kept pace and a common feature of trains that had restaurant or buffet facilities was the use of pre-nationalisation design carriages of these types and many were still prevalent in 1961. Indeed, the ex GWR carriages in the Cornish Riviera set were not replaced until 1961, and possibly only then due to the train having to be diverted over Southern Region lines due to storm damage on the Western route.

October 1 saw the resumption of EMU suburban services around Glasgow following modification to all the sets that had been withdrawn in December 1960. October 9 saw EMUs introduced on the Maidstone-Ashford and Ashford-Ramsgate services. However, electric traction was not expected to start working between Liverpool and Crewe until 1962 despite the continued delivery of electric locomotives which would total over 60 in stock by the year end.

The winter timetable saw the very long-running through trains from Bournemouth to Birkenhead cut short at Wolverhampton and decelerated by introducing additional stops.

At the year end there was a long list of proposed closures outstanding. Whilst the Southern had none active and the LM, ER and NE had eight between them, the Scottish Region listed seven including the Edinburgh suburban circle and the Western proposed 11 including Didcot-Newbury and Whitland to Cardigan.

Observations

On January 25 an attempt to 'steal an engine' occurred when 0-6-0PT 6422 was 'borrowed' from Stafford Road shed and had got as far as Droitwich before control diverted it into a loop 'for investigation' at which point the civilian crew abandoned the engine and ran off.

Those who are natives of the South West of England may recall the 'Westward Television Train' which visited many towns in the region to promote the new television channel with the train being worked by 3440 *City of Truro* whilst on the Western Region and by T9 30120 on the Southern. On completion of its Westward duties 3440 was withdrawn from capital stock.

Also, in 1961, on March 29 the first part of the new National Transport Museum opened in a

A feature of the Weymouth boat trains was the journey from Town Station to the Quay. 0-6-0PT 1368 wends its way gingerly between the parked cars. (T Owen/Colour-Rail)

The final compound locomotive to be withdrawn from capital stock was 41168 in July 1961. It was still resting at Derby works in April 1962. (K Fairey/Colour-Rail.com)

former bus garage in Clapham. Spotters in Brighton were in for a surprise on May 21 when Jubilee 45650 arrived on an excursion from Leicester. It was said to be the first of the Jubilee class to be seen in the town since 1953.

The Royal train made regular appearances throughout the 1960s and in the early years was always allocated steam power with, for example, A4 60033 working through from Walker-on-Tyne to Kings Cross on June 27. At the other end of the scale, despite there now being a surplus of larger engines, less glamorous motive power could still be found handling passenger duties with for example Staveley allocated 4F 44066, employed on two days to work the eight coach 16.38 from Birmingham New Street to Worcester service.

July saw the demise of 4P 41168, this being the last compound engine to remain in stock on the network and was one of 195 of the design built by the LMS between 1924 and 1932. Whilst very efficient, the design did not look modern and yet many of the class were less than 30 years old when withdrawn.

Except for those on the Western Region and D1-D10, most mainline diesel engines did not carry names from new, including the Deltics. In mid-1961 the Midland Region announced a naming programme for D210-36 and named Peak D100 *Sherwood Forester* even though this had been carried by Royal Scot 46112, from which the regimental badges were transferred.

One for the spotters was the arrival at Manchester Victoria on August 26 of Eastleigh-allocated 9F 92206 working in on a train from Bournemouth. It did not return home immediately, being recorded at Bolton two days later.

Football specials were very much still part of the railway scene in 1961 and could on occasions provide unusual motive power, one such being run from Dartford to Bristol via Salisbury on November 25 double-headed by D5009 and D6523 throughout. Unless they were spotters, the Dartford supporters that made the long journey were to be disappointed though, Bristol City won the second-round FA Cup encounter 8-2.

A hardy soul turned out in cold winter weather to record a busy pre-Christmas service on the East Coast mainline on December 22 when 112 trains were recorded. Despite the supposed extensive dieselisation of the route just 34 of the trains had such power with 50 of the others having Pacifics in charge, the remainder being in the hands of V2s and B1s. ∎

3440 City of Truro was used to head the Westward Television train on a promotional west country tour. However, on the first day, February 9, it was at Kensington Olympia and 3440 is just leaving Old Oak Common shed to collect the train.

Britain's Railways in the 1960s

1962
OVERVIEW

The year started with 11,691 steam engines still in stock while the total of diesel and electric engines exceeded 3,000 for the first time. An area of the railways that had seen little change in recent years was that of the size of the workshop capacity. However, the start of the year saw an announcement that Horwich works would cease building new locomotives, whilst rolling stock work would stop at Swindon and Eastleigh. A reduction of 1,830 in the size of the workforce was expected, this to be achieved by the end of 1963. This proved to only be a prelude to the main act as on September 19 a new plan was unveiled which would reduce workshop staff from 50,000 to 38,000 over two years. The plan envisaged that the following works would close: Ashford loco, Bromsgrove, Caerphilly, Darlington, Earlstown, Eastleigh Carriage & Wagon (to be combined with the loco works), Cowlairs, Gorton, Lancing, Stratford, and Wolverhampton.

Also announced were significant regional boundary changes to take effect in 1963. These were to see the Southern losing all of its west country lines beyond Salisbury to the Western which in turn would lose all of its lines in the Midlands, with new boundaries at Banbury, Barnt Green and north of Hereford so all services in mid Wales and the Midlands northwards would become part of the Midland Region.

A pay deal for all staff giving a 3% increase from April 1 was announced as was an increase of 10% in passenger fares as from March 26. On the other side of the equation a 14-day all-line Railrover was introduced with the slogan '10,000 miles for £25'. A 200% rise in the price of a platform ticket, to 3d at some Western Region stations, was bad news for enthusiasts.

A hint of the Beeching proposals came in a report of a speech that he made on March 15 with 'drastic pruning', the elimination of stopping services and wagon load freight being mentioned. With the speech being made in Newcastle, it might not have been a surprise that the loss making Tyneside electrics were singled out for attention despite the fact that the north Tyneside route carried 30,000 passengers daily on a 20 minute frequency service.

The rumour machine was apparently alive and well with a report appearing in the press that Paddington station was to be closed and the Western Region amalgamated with the Southern and Midland, this being rebutted as being 'without foundation'.

In May the Transport Commission announced a new team to manage British Railways, still headed by Dr Beeching. Interestingly, there were area boards rather than regional ones. This was probably in readiness for several boundary changes that were due to take place in 1963 which brought formerly competing lines under a single manager. At a conference in Harrogate a member of the BTC spoke about the Common Market and its opportunities, including the building of a channel tunnel that could be completed in five years. This was to be linked to a new rail route from the north and Midlands to Dover avoiding London.

The year turned out to be a grim one for the steam enthusiast with heavy withdrawals. The process of complete removal of steam from certain areas continued but in respect of changes to mainline power it was primarily the

A rare picture of a South Tyneside electric unit, taken at South Shields. The system was a target for closure and in due course the EMUs found their way to the Southern Region. Colour-Rail.com

1962

2251 class 2286 receives some final attention having just been overhauled at Caerphilly works in March 1962, just six months before it was proposed for closure. (J Wilkinson/Colour-Rail.com)

Western Region that saw major replacement, with steam removed from services to South Wales and the Midlands. For much of the rest of the country it remained a gradual erosion of steam helped by an increased number of line and station closures and reductions in services under the 'economy measures' banner.

Modern Traction Scene

The dawning of the year saw the start of electric working from Liverpool-Crewe by both locos and units with 14 expresses so hauled.

Following the arrival of D1000 in Desert Sand livery in December, D1001 was delivered in maroon followed by others in green. Nearly 300 people entered a competition to vote on the best colour with maroon being chosen, so most of the class carried this from the outset, it also being applied to some Warships in later years.

A new locomotive type appeared on February 5 with electro diesel E6001 starting trials at Eastleigh. Intended mainly for use on electrified routes, it also had a 600hp diesel engine to allow it to operate on non-electrified sidings and branches.

In the rush to remove steam from the Western Region, plans were announced to use the Type 3 Hymeks to work the Paddington-South Wales services from June, replacing Kings and Castles, despite the trains loading to anything up to 14 carriages. Plans were also in hand to introduce the Westerns onto the Paddington-Wolverhampton services most of which were also worked by Kings with the full replacement of steam taking place on September 10.

Less glamorous, but also important in the elimination of steam, was the arrival of a new batch of DEMUs for the Southern, the first being 1301, with their

The first of the 13XX series DEMUs were delivered to the Southern Region and as well as the planned duties on the Oxted route found employment around Ashford. 1307 is seen at Ham Street on 30 June. D Ovenden/Colour-Rail

primary duties being to replace steam on the Oxted line from London.

The woes of the North British Type 2s north of the border continued with D6127 suffering severe fire damage. Support from the manufacturer would no longer be available either as it was announced on April 3 that North British was to be wound up. Also in trouble were the Baby Deltics with only two out of ten being serviceable at Finsbury Park in late April.

The Liverpool-Newcastle services were diagrammed for English Electric Type 4s provided ➤

Britain's Railways in the 1960s 23

Among the locomotives new for the year was English Electric Type 3 D6751 seen here at Sheffield Victoria on February 28, 1962. Colour-Rail.com

by Gateshead and Edge Hill. However, the latter frequently substituted a loco from another depot resulting in Camden and Crewe allocated examples ending up at Newcastle.

The first regular passenger workings by diesels on the South Western Division of the Southern Region took place with the appearance of D65XX on boat train and other duties in the Southampton and Bournemouth areas.

In Scotland, DMUs made redundant by the second phase of the Glasgow electrification project, ousted steam power on duties around Largs and Ardrossan.

The first of yet another new type of diesel locomotive was seen on July 26 at Marylebone when the 900hp Type 1 D8500, which became known as the Clayton, arrived there for inspection. No fewer than 88 had been ordered straight off the drawing board. Although of course not evident at the time, a more significant arrival was that of Brush Type 4 D1500 which was at Crewe for weighing on September 6, the first 20 being destined for the East Coast route.

An overview of the year's deliveries of modern traction showed a sharply reduced intake of just 506 diesel and 20 electric locos. The final two Deltics had arrived and Type 4 power was boosted by D50-67, D151-88, D372-99, D859-65, D1001-14/35-46/8/9 and D1500-2 and Type 3s by D6583-97, D6732-6801 and D7016-61/3. The balance comprised Types 1 and 2 and shunters including the conclusion of the building of 1,193 350hp 0-6-0s with the delivery of D4192. The DMU and EMU delivery programme petered out with an increase of just 33 carriages in total although this hid the fact that some old electric stock was condemned.

Steam Happenings

The 'big four' each had their flagship class, A4s, Duchesses, Merchant Navies and Kings. All were intact at the start of 1962 but the first chink in their elimination came in February with the condemnation of King 6006, with

6006 King George 1 received its last general overhaul at Swindon in February 1960. Two years later it became the first of the class to be condemned. T Owen/Colour-Rail.com

only the Merchant Navies seeing out the year unscathed. However, few would have predicted the elimination of the Kings before the end of the year.

Diesel reliability, particularly on the East Coast route, appeared to be a major problem early in the year with many steam substitutions but things gradually improved month by month.

Notes in magazines recording day to day happenings often only became significant with hindsight. Thus, a note that an A4 had carried out a trial run on a Glasgow to Aberdeen three-hour express gave no clue as to how workings on this route would shine out as a last bastion of steam in the coming years.

The well-known T9 4-4-0s finished regular work on the Southern Region but 30120, instead

1962

Restored T9 120 heads a service train through Berrylands in September 1962. S M Watkins/Colour-Rail.com

of being withdrawn, was repainted in LSWR livery and retained for special duties, but did also find use on timetabled work such as the 12.42 Waterloo-Basingstoke at the end of June.

With the Somerset and Dorset line being targeted for closure, the familiar process of removing traffic from a threatened line commenced with the announcement that the Pines Express would cease to run over the route from September. However, for the third year Bath Green Park received an allocation of 9Fs to work the summer Saturday extras, with 92245 being the first to arrive. It was no co-incidence that 92220 *Evening Star* joined the stud and was employed on the final workings of the service.

With the rundown of regular duties for some classes, they wandered to places where they had never been seen before. Thus, the one and only visit of a Princes Royal, 46203, to Edinburgh Waverley occurred on June 23 when it arrived with a train from Perth. Red-painted Duchess 46244 had appeared a few days earlier on a similar duty.

The implementation of the full electric service on the London Tilbury and Southend line took place removing most steam activity from the area almost overnight. A similar situation was noted in Scotland but in this case on freight duties where 12 EE Type 1s took over all the work of Parkhead shed on July 9. By this time there were only around 50 former Caledonian Railway engines operating compared with nearly 400 at the start of the decade.

Whilst it was reported that steam at Liverpool Lime Street station was now a rarity, just a few miles away as the crow flies, it was diesels that were the rarity on the North Wales coast line, with just two seen in eight hours on July 14. The same could be said of the Cambrian routes where only steam power was recorded on a two day visit. Whilst the Western Region lines in the southwest were by now nearly all diesel worked, the same could not be said of those in the Southern Region. However, one attraction was about to be 'westernised', that being the three ancient Beattie well tanks 30585-7 which were still hard at work at Wadebridge, but their replacements were not diesel but displaced 1366 class 0-6-0PTs 1367-9 which arrived in July.

Liverpool Street station officially became 'steam free' from the start of the winter timetable which also marked the completion of the ending of steam across original GER routes and saw the withdrawal of the last examples of GER steam types.

The ending of the summer timetable heralded the largest withdrawal of steam power ever seen, particularly on the Western Region where 13 Kings, 25 Castles and 34 Halls were condemned en bloc. A notable casualty on the Eastern was the condemnation of a first BR Standard type with 4MT 80103 going due to a cracked frame, this soon being followed by the unique 8P Pacific 71000 *Duke of Gloucester*.

A summary of steam engine withdrawals could be a lengthy affair but the total of 2,924 condemnations, nearly five times greater than the number of diesels arriving, showed the sudden change that occurred. The elimination of classes like the Kings and Schools had also left very few classes intact other than most of the BR Standard types. Things did not bode well for steam in 1963.

Infrastructure and Rolling Stock

With economies being sought across the network, suggestions like a proposal to single a short section of the mainline in ➤

Just a few months before its withdrawal, 71000 Duke of Gloucester was seen at Watford, possibly on its regular duty of the Mid Day Scot, on 31 May. Colour-Rail.com

Britain's Railways in the 1960s

25

Cornwall were typical. This was contemplated to avoid expensive repairs to St Pinnock and East Largin viaducts.

The West Coast electrification project continued, with wiring seen as far south as Tamworth by February although hardly any work had taken place on the Birmingham-Rugby route at that time. Completion as far as Stafford by the year end was the official target and indeed the overhead was energised from November 26. By the autumn masts were appearing as far south as Bletchley. Rebuilding of Coventry station was completed with an opening ceremony held on May 1.

In the west Dr Beeching visited Plymouth on March 28 to officially open the rebuilt Plymouth station, the work having taken six years and cost £1.8m.

The year saw the introduction of the 'auto buffet', this simply being the installation of a vending machine to provide food and drink where a staffed buffet could not be justified. The first use was on the Cambrian Coast Express from Shrewsbury-Aberystwyth.

A new signal box to open was that at Millerhill which went live on May 5 although it appeared to only replace two existing boxes. Meanwhile a new scheme was announced to install colour light signalling on the 25 miles between Hayes & Harlington and Reading.

Thornaby shed, which was not built until 1958, had been designed for conversion for use by diesel traction, and the changeover process started in the spring with a completion planned for October, this coinciding with the arrival of large batch of English Electric Type 3s.

Meanwhile a new diesel depot opened at Shirebrook in early autumn. Cardiff Canton shed shut to steam traction at the end of the summer timetable with its allocation moving to Cardiff East Dock. It was to be completely rebuilt as a diesel depot- a little late to start the work when it already had an allocation of nearly 20 Hymeks.

Services

Closure proposals dominated from the start of the year. A high profile battle loomed over the shutting of 25 stations between Aylesbury and Sheffield although neither Nottingham Victoria nor Sheffield Victoria were included in the proposals. Although 24 lines had been listed for closure in December 1961, a new batch emerged in January 1962 which had over 50 entries. Notable amongst the additions were Plymouth-Launceston, the Newquay branch, all services through Three Cocks, the Severn and Cheddar Valley branches and the whole of the Somerset & Dorset line.

Thornaby shed was built for easy conversion for use as a diesel depot, a process that started in 1962. One of the first of its allocation of BR type 2s mingles amongst the steam power. K Fairey/Colour-Rail.com

Rush hour at Three Cocks on August 8, 1962 with three trains present, a scene soon to be wiped off the railway map in its entirety. T Owen/Colour-Rail.com

1962

A month later additions to the list included the Central Wales line, Hereford-Gloucester and local services between Shrewsbury and Aberystwyth. The following month a major addition was all the Great Central route from Marylebone to Sheffield, not just the stopping services. The May list included Pontypool Road to Neath via Crumlin High Level for the first time whilst the next additions put the Hayling Island Branch and Haltwhistle to Alston in the frame. Two early casualties were Burnmouth-Eyemouth and Rosewell to Galashiels via Peebles, both of which closed on February 5 whilst Bedford-Northampton went on March 5.

Despite most line closures requiring replacement bus services, many did not last, and an example was that provided for the Ashburton and Teign Valley lines. The threatened closure of the Newport valley routes took place at the end of April with 37 stations losing their services.

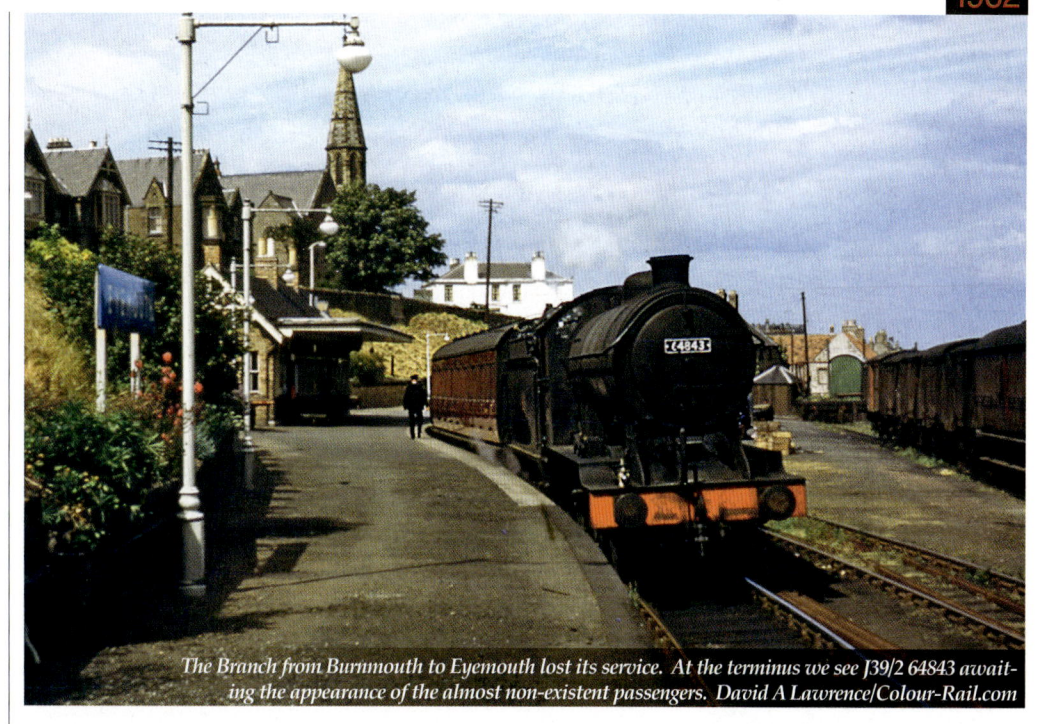

The Branch from Burnmouth to Eyemouth lost its service. At the terminus we see J39/2 64843 awaiting the appearance of the almost non-existent passengers. David A Lawrence/Colour-Rail.com

Eleven lines lost their services on September 19, the first day of the winter timetable, all except two of these being on the Western Region whilst another raft took place in each of October, November and December which, amongst other places, removed Brecon from the railway map. The first 'mutterings' about the viability of services between Oxford and Cambridge started towards the end of the year. Occasionally closure proposals were refused and one such stay of execution was for the Gloucester-Chalford auto train service.

The MP for the Isle of Wight got wind of discussions about the complete withdrawal of rail services on the island. The Minister of Transport admitted that there had been discussions with the local bus company but that seven years notice would be given if the plan went ahead.

Dr Beeching had required all regions to implement service cuts as an economy measure. An example of these was the Bristol area plan which saw widespread reductions in services from March 5 to save £0.25m. Typical of these were to be seen on the Severn Beach line where services were cut from 14 per day to six and all small stations in the Bristol area were closed on Sundays.

The 1962 summer timetable saw the spread of diesel power to the North & West route from Newport to Shrewsbury with services accelerated by around 30 minutes. This also eliminated the last major steam duty between Newton Abbot and Bristol.

East Coast accelerations introduced the six hour timing for the Flying Scotsman. Back in 1862 the schedule had been 10 ½ hours.

On the downside as far as passengers were concerned was a considerable pruning of summer Saturday dated trains, especially on the Southern Region.

The advent of the winter timetable on the Southern saw many cuts in services including the introduction of 'bustitution' at Weymouth where boat train passengers were bussed between the town and quay stations. To allow electrification work to be undertaken on the West Coast route to Manchester, services to Euston were reduced and to compensate additional trains were run from St Pancras over the Midland route.

An innovative new freight service started trials. This, known as the 'Night Importer', comprised three trains which ran overnight from London Victoria Docks to Liverpool, the North East and Scotland. The autumn saw the ➤

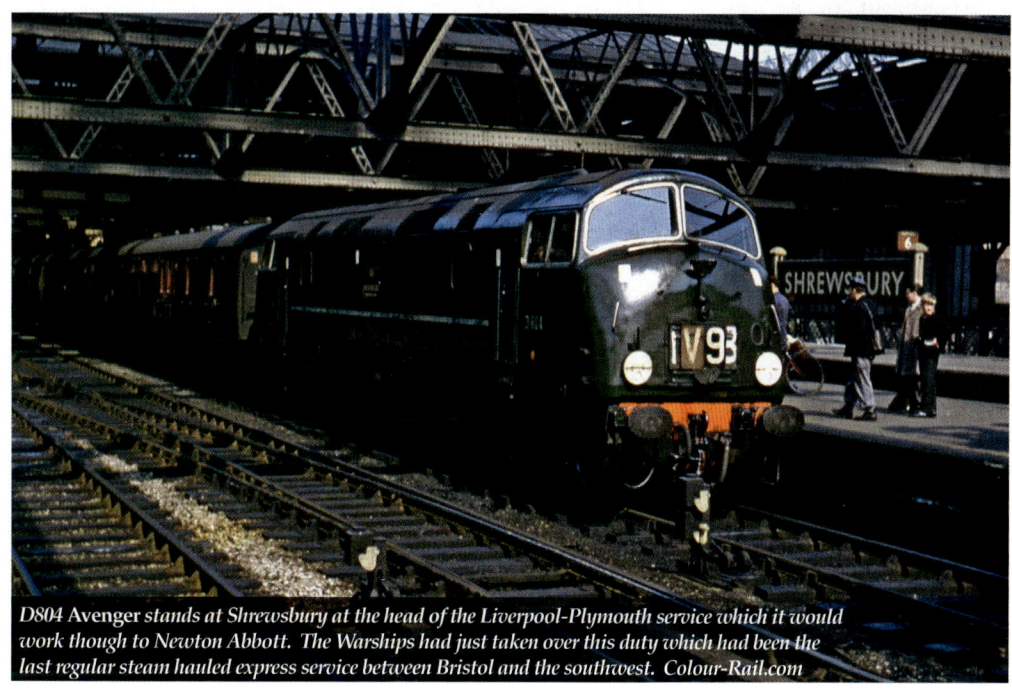

D804 Avenger stands at Shrewsbury at the head of the Liverpool-Plymouth service which it would work though to Newton Abbott. The Warships had just taken over this duty which had been the last regular steam hauled express service between Bristol and the southwest. Colour-Rail.com

Britain's Railways in the 1960s

1962

An engine to be noted was 8F 48424, not here on its home turf at Hagley, but certainly when it appeared at Lostock Hall in March. R Siviter/Colour-Rail.com

start of a weekly service conveying new cars between Oxford and Scotland, the return working conveying commercial vehicles and tractors. In the early 1960s the circus still came to town by special train and when Bertram Mills visited Hull on May 20 no fewer than four trains were required to convey the performers and animals.

The line from Redditch to Ashchurch had been proposed for closure with a decision awaited, when at the end of September the civil engineer refused to be responsible for the safety of the track, causing all services to be suspended from October 1.

For the first time no passenger trains operated on the Western Region on Christmas day.

Observations

Excursions for special events continued in the main to be steam worked with the Grand National on March 31, 1962 bringing 13 specials to Aintree. All were steam worked with named locomotives predominating. Starting points were the London area through to Glasgow, across to Cleethorpes and up to Newcastle. B1 61065 from Hull was perhaps the most notable attendee. An 8F at Lostock Hall shed (Preston) would hardly have got the local spotters excited but vigilance was always important, as it would have been easy to ignore 48424 which visited on March 5, but reference to the Ian Allan shed book would have shown that its home was Stourbridge Junction, making it one not to be missed.

Western Region power wandering even further afield was Bristol allocated Jubilee 45690 which got as far as Glasgow on April 20. At the other end of the country another Jubilee, 45660 of Shrewsbury shed managed to get to Exeter when it worked the 3.32pm Bristol-Penzance parcels.

A Battle of Britain enjoyed a day out on a football excursion on November 3 when 34087 worked from Bournemouth to Coventry via Oxford and was serviced at Nuneaton shed.

Proving that new is not always best, the Royal Wessex service from Waterloo to Weymouth had been using the latest BR Mk1 carriages that only seated six people per compartment, leading to overcrowding on this popular service. To overcome the problem the sets were replaced by Bulleid designed stock which seated eight.

Since its opening, the Lickey incline at Bromsgrove had reverberated to the sound of almost every train ascending the bank being worked by two or more engines. Following trials with Peak D40 early in the year, diesel engines were now allowed to take up to 12 coaches up the bank unassisted as well as certain freights

Another survey (see 1961) was carried out on the East Coast mainline on December 21 and showed that little modernisation progress had occurred in the last 12 months, with diesel use up to 43 trains from 34, but with an almost identical number of steam turns being recorded. A sign that regional independence might be under threat could be seen on the Western, which had for several years operated most front line express services with stock in chocolate and cream livery, but from mid-1962 new stock deliveries were in the standard maroon, with this quickly being allocated to Cornish Riviera duties amongst others. Loose coupled (i.e. unbraked) freight trains remained a major feature of railway operation and the newly introduced diesels had been found to be unable to provide enough brake force on some duties to prevent runaways. To overcome this problem 1962 saw the arrival of the first brake tenders, effectively huge concrete blocks on wheels with braking operated from the loco, these being coupled in front of it when working heavy trains on some routes. December 1962 brought with it dense fog and freezing temperatures which caused considerable disruption across particularly the north of England and on December 29 heavy snow struck much of the country, a portent of a grim start to 1963. The fog and ice saw overnight services from London to Glasgow arriving over seven hours late on December 5/6. ∎

Insufficient brake force on some diesels saw the introduction of the brake tender with an example seen here at Cargo Fleet in June. Colour-Rail.com

1963 OVERVIEW

British Railways opened the year under the new management system announced in 1962 with Dr Beeching as chairman of the British Railways Board. One of its responsibilities was to manage its Road Motor Division which operated more than 15,000 vehicles and this was headed by a Mr G White who had previously worked for the Post Office.

Another change was that the Pullman Car Company was merged into BR at the start of the year. To complete the picture of change the previously mentioned region boundary changes also applied from January 1. The opening motive power stock comprised 3,861 diesel and electric locomotives, 5,427 DMU and EMU cars and 8,767 steam locomotives.

Rarely can the weather be relevant to an overview, but the winter of 1962/3 was to be a major factor in how the railways performed in the first quarter of the year where the low temperatures found modern traction wanting. An unfortunately mistimed report in the railway press stated that Western Region chemists had found that UK winters were not cold enough, the usual thawing and refreezing that took place being the major cause of problems with frozen points. Whilst conditions eased from mid-March it was to be April before the modern traction fleet availability returned to normal.

A Design Exhibition was held in London from February 26 to March 23 which contained a full size mock-up of proposed new carriage designs along with ideas for new uniforms, liveries, station design and equipment and even new cross-channel ferries.

The much anticipated Beeching report was published on March 27. The government was said to have accepted the majority of the proposals which included the closure of around one third of the network, but also said that it might insist that some of the lines be retained with subsidies paid. As well as the removal of competing routes such as the former Southern lines in Devon and Cornwall and most of the ex-Great Central system, places such as Skegness, Stranraer and the Isle of Wight would no longer be served by rail along with the more remote parts of Wales, Scotland and South-West England. More than 3,000 stations were listed for closure. In Scotland Inverness would be the northern outpost of the system with Wales losing all north-south lines except the North & West route. Coaching and freight stock totals were to see a significant reduction but there was still to be a considerable expansion of the locomotive fleet. Less well publicised at the time were the positive ideas put forward such as the running of long distance 'block' freight trains. There was very vocal protest from both the unions and the public in areas where major service cuts were proposed.

The summer timetable, whilst containing many fewer services than previously, showed that over 200 more journeys were timed at an average speed above 60mph bringing the total to over 500 with 22 at over 70mph. At a press conference in November plans were announced for a recasting and speeding up of services to the west country on the former GWR route. More worrying was the statement that only one route to the west would be needed in the future and the Southern from Exeter to Plymouth was clearly stated as up for closure. Freight concentration depots were planned for four locations in the area.

An interesting twist on the modern day advanced ticket went on sale, this being the day/night rider ticket which offered fares of ➤

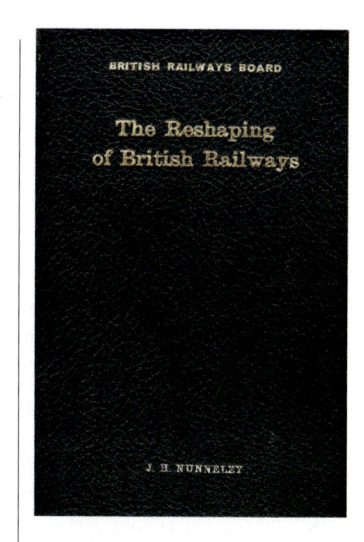

J H Nunneley was one of the small management team that worked with Dr Beeching on the preparation of his report and each received a leather bound copy of the document as seen here. Colour-Rail.com

As well as running trains, British Railways was a major operator of lorries and typical of the period was this Ford Thames Trader seen at Wadebridge. David A Lawrence/Colour-Rail.com

Britain's Railways in the 1960s

The ex GWR railcars became extinct in the year. Here we see W23 at Tenbury Wells. Colour-Rail.com

£3-3s/£2 respectively for travel on specified trains from London to Glasgow or Edinburgh, the twist being that they could only be purchased from one hour before departure subject to seats being available.

Modern Traction Scene

Losses on the Tyneside electric system were addressed early in the year with the January 7 seeing all EMUs on South Tyne services withdrawn and replaced by DMUs, but frequencies were increased to every 20 minutes instead of half hourly. Usage of the electrified system was said to have fallen from 3.5 million journeys in 1956 to 2.5million in 1961. The redundant stock was to be transferred to the Southern Region.

The term Modern Traction is used to describe all forms of diesel and electric power but not all of it was anything like new. One type to disappear from the system was the GWR railcar with the last one in stock being No. 32.

The first demonstrations of the new electric stock for the Clacton line took place in February. These express units carried maroon livery in the same style as the new coaching stock.

New orders were placed for a large number of Brush Type 4s taking the total expected to 362, along with 20 more EE Type 3s and a new design of diesel hydraulic, this being a 650 hp 0-6-0 for shunting and transfer duties, the initial order being for 26. An order for a further 30 was placed before delivery of the first of the class. The first batch of Brush Type 4s started to make their mark on the East Coast route from March onwards. Orders announced in September were for 100 3,300hp electric locomotives to complete the West Coast scheme and 108 4-car EMUs for the Southern Region.

The shade of green paint used on the DMU fleet had varied considerably, being anything from a bright Malachite to dark green. The year saw the adoption of one of the darker shades as standard as vehicles passed through works for repaint. The Southern Region started to receive a further batch of 4 CEP units in March but these, like all other Southern EMUs, were in the lighter shade of green as used on their coaching stock.

March saw the arrival of the first EE Type 3s on the Western Region. Whilst some trials and training were carried out from Bristol, the new locos were all allocated to South Wales depots and with their rapid rate of delivery soon made inroads to the steam freight monopoly in the principality. In addition, Westerns were arriving in large numbers in the area, replacing the Hymeks on the

The Baby Deltics spent much of the year in store before being returned to their maker for rebuilding. D5903 and a friend did plenty of sunbathing at Stratford in August. T Owen/Colour-Rail.

30 Britain's Railways in the 1960s

Paddington and other express services.

The first use of diesel power over the former Southern lines in Devon and Cornwall was noted as early as April with both Warships and D63XX being involved. In the autumn Brush Type 4s started to replace Westerns on Wolverhampton-London services as these were now the responsibility of the Midland Region.

One advantage of modern traction was that it could work long distances, unlike the relatively frequent engine changes seen on many steam-worked services. The use of pairs of D6500s on the Cliffe to Uddingston cement train as far as York had been going on for some time but a new freight service from Glasgow to Gosford Green near Coventry brought Polmadie-based English Electric Type 1s to the Midlands from April.

The Clayton diesels introduced in 1962, like other classes, suffered from teething problems but from around April 1963 they started appearing in quantity across southern Scotland, mainly on freight duties, but they did have some passenger work. Some classes took longer to show their weaknesses. The Hymeks were a case in point, where metal fatigue issues came to light leading to the down rating of some class members and a suspension to deliveries. However, that did not stop them making an appearance on Paddington-Worcester services from mid-May.

The Metrovick diesels had given trouble ever since their introduction and like other less successful types, were found employment hidden away from the main line, in this case in Cumbria with all arriving there by June. At the same time in Scotland the experimental rebuilding of a North British Type 2 with a Paxman engine saw D6123 enter service so fitted and painted in two tone green. Yet another problematical class, the D59XX Baby Deltics were returned to English Electric for modification.

Hymek availability gave rise to yet more problems with several steam engines being taken out of store to cover duties and plans to completely dieselise Worcester-Paddington duties had to be put on hold. Many Westerns were also removed from traffic in mid-November for transmission modifications.

What turned out to be the last design of DMU based on the Mk1 carriage commenced delivery in June from Swindon, these being four-car cross country sets. Apart from some of the Scottish Region units, also built at Swindon, these were the only DMUs to have front end corridor connections. All were allocated to the Western Region and were put to work on long distance routes such as Cardiff to Plymouth.

A sign of things to come was the storage of two diesel railbuses at Perth, these not yet being five years old. Also condemned was former LMS 10000 and Southern diesels 10201-3.

Polmadie allocated EE Type 1s were regular visitors to the Midlands and D8125 and another were photographed at Rugby. Colour-Rail.com

Compared to the previous year a reduction of steam power by 1,717 engines was relatively modest. The number of new locomotives was also down at just under 400. New Type 4s into service were D57, D189-93 D1015-26, D1030/1/47/50-73, D1503-49, and D1682-97/9 whilst Type 3 deliveries comprised D6787-95, D6802-D6911 and D7062/4-97. The only other types delivered were many BR designed Type 2s and the 900hp Claytons so at least there was now some standardisation taking place. The total was made up with 16 electrics for the West Coast route. Only the Swindon built DMUs bolstered stock whilst new EMUs went to the Eastern and Southern Regions.

Steam Happenings

With the boundary changes that occurred on January 1 the Midland Region took over a large stock of ex GWR motive power and ten engine sheds in the former 84 and 89 depot groups. Likewise, the Western took over all the 72 Southern depots except Salisbury. There was no immediate change in operations or indeed motive power, although as time moved on many GW types were replaced by LMS or BR Standard designs on the Midland, whilst on the Western Region gradual dieselisation saw off much of the Southern motive power. A typical early example of de-westernisation in the newly acquired Midland area was the exchange of four 28XX freight engines for a similar number of 9Fs between Banbury and Slough sheds.

The preservation movement was under way and the Bluebell Railway had already restored several locomotives. Subject to being 'fit to run', BR allowed them to work on the network to haul special trains such as E4 473 *Birch Grove*, which worked a special from London to Haywards Heath on March 31.

The severe weather encountered during the first three months of the ▶

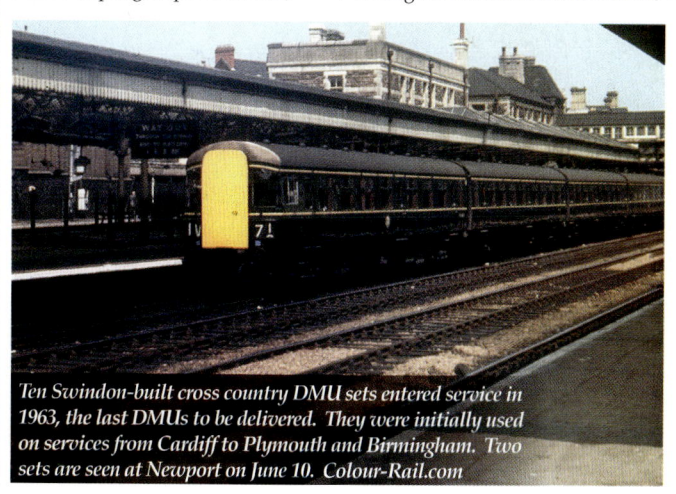

Ten Swindon-built cross country DMU sets entered service in 1963, the last DMUs to be delivered. They were initially used on services from Cardiff to Plymouth and Birmingham. Two sets are seen at Newport on June 10. Colour-Rail.com

Britain's Railways in the 1960s

The year saw the withdrawals of the final engines that had been inherited from the Caledonian Railway. One of their final passenger duties saw 54465 employed extensively on railtours seen here on April 23, 1963 at Blairgowrie. R Patterson/Colour-Rail.com

year put a brake on some steam withdrawals with none taking place in Scotland in February for instance. And stored engines were returned to traffic across the country. Push-Pull working, a major feature of branch lines across the country for many years, only operated on a handful of lines by 1963, mostly on the former Southern Region, but Seaton Junction to Stamford and Gloucester to Chalford were other examples.

Despite all of the class being withdrawn in 1962, King 6018 was reinstated in April for use on a final commemorative railtour which ran from Birmingham to Swindon on April 28. The engine had been used on local duties for a few days prior to the run.

The elimination of older steam classes led to much less variety in engines at some sheds. For example, West Auckland had an allocation consisting solely of Q6 0-8-0s and BR Standard 4MTs. However, this was not to last long as the shed closed at the end of the year, its work having been taken over by seven diesels based at Thornaby.

Despite the huge influx of diesel shunters over the years many pilot and shunting duties remained steam worked, for instance at Birkenhead docks where 47160 was at work, with Jinties at high profile stations such as Crewe, Chester, and Carlisle. Indeed, the Midland Region, away from the main lines, was still very much a steam railway. At Preston on Whit Sunday, an evening observation recorded no fewer than 71 returning excursions of which just ten had diesel power.

Showing that Eastern steam was really under threat was the announcement that all steam engine overhauls would cease at Doncaster works at the end of August.

Most of the A4s allocated to Kings Cross were moved to New England from the start of the summer timetable which saw a major decrease in steam workings on the route. However, October marked the end for the A4s on most of the East Coast route as five were withdrawn whilst the other five lived to fight another day being transferred to Scotland and their new-found fame on the Glasgow-Aberdeen service. Those remaining at Gateshead also soon moved north of the border.

The Western Region saw fit to withdraw the first West Country and Battle of Britain Pacifics, all of

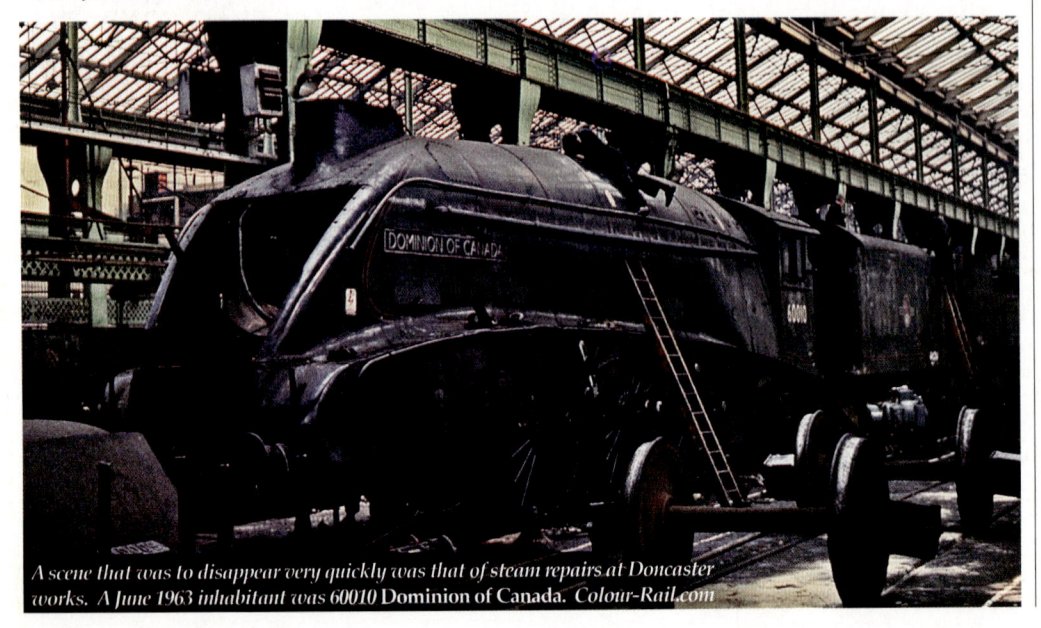

A scene that was to disappear very quickly was that of steam repairs at Doncaster works. A June 1963 inhabitant was 60010 Dominion of Canada. Colour-Rail.com

Britain's Railways in the 1960s

1963

4073 Caerphilly Castle was handed over to the care of the Science Museum in June 1961 at Paddington, but it would be a further two years before it went on display at Clapham. Colour-Rail.com

Looking to have plenty going on, this was Grantham shed in April 1963. Two months later it would lie silent as steam territory receded northwards on the East Coast route. K Fairey/Colour-Rail

One of a diminishing number of push-pull services operating was that from Wareham to Swanage. M7 30108 heads out of the terminus in August. Colour-rail.com

which were in original condition. Rather than first withdrawals, November saw the last of 737 ex-Caledonian Railways engines on BR books at nationalisation being condemned.

March depot closed to steam in November. Whilst most of the allocation was withdrawn, the Britannia Pacifics were transferred to the Midland Region, a move that would see the whole class working there shortly.

Infrastructure

The Tinsley project to build a new yard and depot progressed with the depot opening during the year, well ahead of the completion of the yard. Carlisle yard was completed as was a new facility at Lamesley near Gateshead taking the name of Tyne Yard, but work on a new yard at Stourton was suspended. A new signalling centre at Healey Mills also opened replacing six other boxes.

The second phase of the Transport Museum at Clapham opened to the public on May 29, this comprising the so called large exhibits such as 4073 *Caerphilly Castle* and the prototype Deltic.

The Euston Hotel closed on May 13 to be demolished as part of the Euston reconstruction project, its claim to fame being that it was the first railway hotel in the world. As electrification work moved southwards, various restrictions were put in place such as the closing of Coventry station on Sundays. The first electrically hauled passenger train reached Lichfield on October 21. The new signalbox at Nuneaton was commissioned in the same month.

Landore opened as a diesel depot on May 6 following a complete rebuild. Caerphilly works was an early victim of the workshop rationalisation project with formal closure coming in July. One of the main sheds on the East Coast mainline, Grantham, closed on June 17.

Despite the threat to rail services on the Isle of Wight, heavy maintenance on Ryde Pier saw it closed to rail traffic from the end of September with a planned reopening in April 1964.

Some locations hung to life by a thread following rationalisation, one such being Hellifield Station in North Yorkshire which was said to portray an air of utter desolation, with all the yards becoming overgrown and the shed empty. The refreshment rooms had been closed for four years. The only happenings were stops by the sparse passenger service and freight rumbling through; the beginning of the battle for the survival of the S&C line had arrived.

As noted above, the quantity

Britain's Railways in the 1960s   33

of steam withdrawals was down compared to the previous year, but considerable inroads to the large passenger classes had been made with only the Merchant Navies and Britannias intact. Whilst steam power was still active across most of the same areas as in 1962, in many cases it now hung by a thread. On the Southern the 'no steam' line was gradually moving westward and was roughly to a line from London-Brighton although still M7s hung onto some branch line work in Kent. On the Western it was still only the area south of Plymouth that was (almost) steam free. From East Anglia the line of diesel-only operation was rapidly approaching the East Coast mainline and moving into Lincolnshire and the Midland lines south of Derby were also seeing steam squeezed out. Much of northeast and northwest England along with central and north Wales had seen little change, whilst in Scotland steam was still quite active on the east side and across the central belt.

Services
An early economy measure announced was that the movement of livestock by rail in small numbers was uneconomic and that locations handling such traffic were to be reduced from 2,493 to just 232.

The year had seen the publication of the Beeching report, and such was the expectation on its recommendations that new closure proposals had been put on hold at the start of the year. However, closure via the back door continued, with for instance all Sunday trains being withdrawn on the Great Central lines to allow 'essential maintenance' to take place.

Churston was the junction station for the branch to Brixham that saw out its final days worked by a single car DMU. W55034 was in charge in June 1962. Colour-rail.com

The Western Region promised accelerated services on the Worcester line from the start of the summer timetable when it was planned that Hymeks would take over on the route.

A new-style contract was signed with oil producer Petrofina to convey all its UK production by rail in company-owned wagons and it was joined by Mobil and Gulf during the year.

While 1962 had seen a reduction of the number of carriages on trains out of Broad Street and the new year brought timetable revisions, reducing service frequency on the route to Richmond with weekend services also pruned. Rumours of complete closure also emerged.

The regional boundary changes included the Vale of Rheidol line at Aberystwyth which was now part of the Midland Region. This move, combined with the Beeching proposals, worried the local council to the extent that it approached BR to discuss purchase. The line was indeed loss making and proposals

All rail facilities were proposed for withdrawal at Neyland leading to high unemployment in the area. 7829 Ramsbury Manor, just 13 years old at the time, heads out of Neyland on May 25. R Patterson/Colour-Rail.com

Britain's Railways in the 1960s

to improve the situation, such as 'one engine in steam', came to the fore.

One of the few lines to lose its services in the first half of the year was the Brixham branch in Devon.

For the first time the summer timetable contained no long distance services over the Somerset & Dorset route, a sure sign that it was being softened up for closure. However, of 17 trains that had gone that way in 1962 only 12 ran via the alternative lines in 1963. One magazine of the time reported that complete closure had been agreed by the TUCC to take place on September 30 whilst at the same time advertising a farewell railtour for October 6. However, at least the closure notice proved to be a little premature. Another line to receive a stay of execution was that from Haltwhistle to Alston where the cost of upgrading the road system to be 'winter proof' was said to be far more than that of running the branch. Nottingham-Rugby was another rejection as was St Blazey to Newquay, but eight lines did close in July and August. September closures were more drastic including Crewe to Wellington and the Severn Valley line with 29 stations shut. The impact of some closures could not be under estimated with that of Neyland shed being quoted where, as all staff were made redundant, most people in the village were out of work as it was the only source of employment. At the other end of the scale Stewarts Lane shed in London also closed.

From the summer timetable most express services on the Waterloo-Portsmouth line were increased to 12 carriages. However, several platforms needed to be extended and at the outset, if any passenger chose the wrong part of the train, they would be stuck as there was no provision for pulling up.

The coming of the winter timetable saw many service reductions. In some cases, facilities were also cut with for instance no catering vehicles on any service in Cornwall, these being detached/added at Plymouth. The much photographed Hemyock branch closed to passengers, but the milk traffic was to survive for a few years yet. Another line that had attracted attention due to it being the last one worked by the diminutive 'Terrier' 0-6-0Ts was the Hayling Island branch, this being closed in November. Indeed, the pace of closures was hotting up with 26 lines affected in the closing months of the year.

By the year end closure notifications because of the Beeching proposals were appearing throughout the country. However, as objections were lodged in most cases, the proposed closing dates were then postponed awaiting hearing by the relevant TUCC and then formal sanctioning by the Transport Minister.

Observations

The Z class tanks which had been a feature of the banking duties at Exeter were replaced at the start of the year by W class 2-6-4Ts, some arriving before the official takeover of the area by the Western Region. They did not last long with 0-6-0 pannier tanks being substituted before the year end.

Despite freezing weather many enthusiasts turned out to witness the last run of 60103 *Flying Scotsman* which worked the 1.15 Kings Cross-Leeds service as far as Doncaster on January 15, this being its last duty having been sold to Alan Pegler for preservation. It was operational again in its guise as 4472 by April.

The heavy snow which had fallen particularly in the south on December 29, 1962 was followed by several weeks of sub-zero temperatures and more snowfalls. Many lines were completely blocked for a period but more problematic in the long term was the susceptibility of the steam heating boilers on the diesels to freezing up. This resulted in many services reverting to steam haulage, or in some cases with a steam diesel combination, with the former there just to provide the heating. It also led to many unusual class workings just to keep services running such as the arrival of Duchess 46220 at Bristol on a train from Crewe. On the Midland diesels were transferred to freight duties with no fewer than 12 different Jubilees being reported on trains into St Pancras in January.

Typical of conditions in the north, the Settle & Carlisle line was closed for five days after the night sleeper became stranded in January, but further snow saw it out of action from February 6 -23. The same level of snowfall saw five trains and three engines buried in drifts around Tavistock.

So many steam engines were arriving in Plymouth that Laira shed could not cope with them all and many had to be serviced at the former Southern shed at Friary. A notable visitor on January 23 was Crewe North based Britannia 70052 which arrived nearly four hours late on the 12.5pm from Manchester. The Southern Region fared little better with the Atlantic Coast Express being 3 ½ hours late ➤

Trade looks brisk at North Hayling as 32650 arrives on November 2 but the line was doomed due to the condition of the long trestle bridge that gave rail access to the island. G F Bloxham/Colour-Rail.com

You can feel the cold as 1009 County of Carmarthen *brings its passenger train into Bristol Temple Meads whilst substituting for a diesel on January 23, 1963. It was withdrawn a few days later. Colour-Rail.com*

Britain's Railways in the 1960s

1963

Princess Margaret Rose stands at Crewe having been repainted ready for display by Billy Butlin at his holiday camps. Colour-Rail.com

into Waterloo on January 3 and many electric services struggled as the third rail became encased in ice and snow. On the Eastern Region things got so bad that the timetable had to be thinned due to lack of motive power, whilst the Waverley route in Scotland was blocked by snow on four occasions in the month. The West Coast route was similarly affected with steam to the fore.

Northampton shed managed to get hold of B1 61257 from Thornaby and used it on services to Euston. Unusually Scotland avoided much of the snow but the line from Glasgow to Stranraer was closed for several days and some passengers had to be rescued by helicopter from a stranded train.

The year saw the first sales of locomotives to Butlins for display at their holiday camps with 46203 *Princess Margaret Rose* passing into their ownership.

Despite the availability by now of a considerable number of diesels, the Schoolboy's Football International at Wembley on April 27, 1963 produced 11 specials all of which were steam worked whilst more exciting for those living in Birmingham was an FA Cup semi-final between Manchester and Southampton that brought nine Bulleid Pacifics to Snow Hill on the same day.

Just how far should one have to travel in a DMU? An excursion from Wolverhampton pushed the limits on Easter Sunday by working through to Ramsgate. The run proved too much for one car which caught fire near London. However, in days when health and safety were not quite so prominent, once the fire was extinguished and the coach locked out of use, the train continued its perambulations and still managed to arrive on time.

The replacement of the Z class tanks on banking duties at Exeter found the alternatives lacking. On a wet March 28, a cement train headed by 3812 had Standard 4MTs 80038/64 attached at the front with 2MT 41320 and W 31916 on the ear to surmount the bank from St Davids to Central station.

August 8, 1963 is a date that went down in history, this being when 'The Great Train Robbery' as it became known, took place at Sears Crossing near Cheddington in Buckinghamshire with the train being hauled by D326.

Giving a sense of the size of some dock operations at the time was the recording of 20 350 hp shunters stabled within Newport docks, this being greater for instance than the shunting requirement at Southampton.

A survey of summer Saturday trains at Shap found that 50% remained steam hauled, apparently little different to the situation in 1961.

And a high-tech (for the time) computerised parking system was installed at Plymouth station. It counted cars entering and leaving and automatically displayed a 'car park full' notice.

The annual parking ticket price was set at £8.

One of many steam-hauled services over Shap on summer Saturdays sees 45601 British Guiana heading north in July. A E R Cope/Colour-Rail.com

Britain's Railways in the 1960s

1964 OVERVIEW

The year opened with 4,060 diesel and 194 electric locomotives in stock with 7,050 steam engines on the books. However, over 1000 of these steam locomotives had been put into store by the start of February.

There were two key dates in the year. Firstly, on May 28 BR unveiled its XP64 project with the running of an eight coach train between Marylebone and High Wycombe composed of prototype carriages and headed by D1733. The carriages were of integral construction and some 5.5 tons lighter than existing designs and were mounted on a new B4 bogie. The locomotive was painted blue and carried the now iconic double arrow symbol with the stock in blue and grey livery. It was due to enter service on The Talisman on June 15 but did not materialise.

The second was October 15. This saw the election of the Labour Party under Harold Wilson. The party had campaigned against the closures proposed by Beeching and said that it would halt the programme if it got into power. Whilst it might have been more pro railway than the Conservatives, the campaign promise was not kept, and the contraction of the system continued.

Despite the contraction of freight services, the BR board authorised the purchase of 1,925 motor vehicles and 1,025 trailers at a cost of £2.5m for delivery before the end of 1965.

A scheme to remove the last steam hauled expresses from BR was announced detailing plans to electrify the route to Bournemouth using the established third rail system. This would require a quantity of new EMUs to be built but also utilised existing loco hauled stock that would be included in EMU formations.

New ticket offerings continued to be developed, one such being the East Anglian Ranger giving six days unlimited travel in that area for £4.

Announcements of orders for new engines ceased to be made public once the BRB took over from the BTC. However, during 1964 it emerged that a further 130 Brush Type 4s were expected and the BR Type 2s would extend up to D7677, whilst the EE Type 3s would go up to D6999 and that a further nine would become D6600-8. Finally, more electro diesels similar to E6001-6 would be delivered as E6007-36.

The year had seen the largest closure programme ever and the continued thinning of steam power although few areas had been added to the steam no go list seen previously.

Modern Traction Scene

Brush Type 4s were set to have a major impact during 1964 with deliveries running at three to four units per week at the start of the year.

On the Southern Region, EMU ➤

A second batch of electro diesels were ordered during the year including E6013 seen here at Waterloo. Colour-Rail.com

The new British Railways image was portrayed by D1733 and a train of prototype rolling stock. Colour-Rail.com

Britain's Railways in the 1960s

Such was the pace of the building of the Brush Type 4s that the paint shop at the Brush plant could not keep pace, with several examples being sent to Derby Works in undercoat for completion. D1751 is seen on June 28, 1964 along with D1748 and another. T Owen/Colour-Rail.com

stock dating from before the war had always been used on Bognor services but 4BEP and 4CEP units were transferred in early in the year, with the older units moved to the Portsmouth line.

The continuing misfortune of the D61XX diesels found large numbers of them in store on the Scottish Region in February.

A new batch of Claytons was split between the Eastern and North Eastern Regions with Thornaby being an early beneficiary, but as seen on several occasions the roll out of diesel power was not moving as fast as the authorities wished, with the originally planned December 1962 elimination of steam at that shed now planned for May, nearly 18 months late.

Having taken delivery of the final build of DMUs, the contraction in branch services was now rendering stock redundant and the first condemnations came in the form of 1955-built Derby lightweight units.

Most railbuses were also laid aside although none had been withdrawn in the early part of the year.

The Hampshire scheme DEMUs, introduced in the late 1950s, proved to be a great success and passenger numbers had grown to the point where overcrowding was becoming a problem. Therefore, the transfer of several units to replace steam-worked services on the Central Division was not viewed positively by folks in Hampshire where some steam duties were set to return, and train lengths cut.

A process of cascading diesel engines was starting and would become more common as time went by. An example was the arrival of D1570-3 at Holbeck which replaced D189-92 on trains to Kings Cross.

Many of the East Coast EE Type 4s were also replaced by the more powerful Brush engines, which released them to work previously steam diagrammed parcels and freight duties.

Banking duties at Bromsgrove changed from steam to diesel in mid-year, initially with EE Type 3s but later with Hymeks.

Whilst the changes in regional boundaries saw little immediate change for the locomotive fleet, in the case of DMUs, of which there were many at Tyseley when it moved from the Western to the Midland, the 'W' prefix on each carriage had to be removed and replaced by an 'M'. This was initially done quite crudely with the W painted out and a stencilled M put in its place.

The Western Region railbuses had become redundant when the services that they worked from Kemble were withdrawn. However, two were then transferred to work the Bodmin branch.

With more DMUs becoming available as services reduced, the winter timetable saw services in areas such as around Birmingham Snow Hill and Preston to Blackpool being converted and steam ousted. However, the plan to convert most Cambrian line duties to DMUs at that time failed to materialise.

July had seen the emergence of the last new class of diesel locomotive for a few years when D9500 and friends entered service at Bristol. The saga of this class would unveil and be completed

With time running out, Exmouth Junction shed just about clung to life until the year end. Here 41291 and a DMU were resident on December 19, 1964. G Parry Collection/Colour-Rail.com

D191 was one of four Peaks to be displaced from turns to Kings Cross from Leeds by Brush Type 4s. It is seen here on one such duty in 1963. D Ovenden/Colour-Rail.com

in painting the shed allocation in full on the buffer beam. However, St Rollox works had ceased steam repairs and was said to be undergoing conversion to carry out diesel overhauls.

Crewe continued with steam overhauls south of the border but applied a very different standard of finish, using 'economy' liveries, i.e. unlined green or black which were not enhanced when they stopped applying a high gloss finish. Horwich turned out its last steam repair, 48756, on May 6. Eastleigh, as well as catering for the diminishing Southern fleet, started to take in Standard classes from other regions. When out-shopped their running-in turns provided some rare sightings for spotters in the area such as 75002 from Machynlleth. Swindon also had a brief period of dealing with foreign engines with Stanier, Ivatt and Standard 2-6-0s being the usual fare.

With the closing of sheds and the large reductions in steam power, if a stand-in was required for a diesel engine it could travel well into 'foreign territory' before another suitable engine could be provided. An instance of this was the use of Hall 7912 from Banbury to Nottingham Victoria when the diesel for the Bournemouth-York train failed. However, Halls became regular visitors to Nottingham on summer Saturday Bournemouth-Bradford workings, quite often handing over to a Holbeck allocated Jubilee. Class 9Fs were also in use on passenger duties in the area. Instead of a Hall, Grange 6858 was provided on a Bournemouth West-Leeds service on August 12, said to be the first Grange class to visit Leicester. However, due to no replacement engine being available the interloper made it as far north as Huddersfield before being replaced.

Observations at Blackpool in March and April showed that more trains were steam hauled than had been the case a year earlier.

Gradual changes in motive power occurred which often only became apparent when looking back to former years. One such was the replacement of ex-GW classes by BR Standards on the Cambrian lines, with most services on the route to Pwllheli being so worked by mid-1964, mainly by 75XXX and 82XXX classes, but Manors (one of the few steam classes still intact at this time) always worked the Cambrian Coast Express from Aberystwyth to Shrewsbury.

One of the more unusual reallocations was that of A2 Pacifics to Polmadie shed where they found employment mainly on stopping services out of Glasgow St Enoch station. When

over the next five years. They arrived at a time when reports of diesel shunters being under employed in various parts of the country were already commonplace.

Electric units transferred from Tyneside started to enter traffic on the Southern from August.

The pace of locomotive deliveries was little different to that of the previous year totalling 408 diesels and just six electrics as follows:- D1027-9/32-4, D1550-1645/98, D1700/1/7-72/4/91/3/4, D5240-98, D6887-98, D6912-50, D7098-D7100, D7500-18/20/82-97, D8567-D8611, D9500-16/8-24 and E3084/5/92/4/5/7. No new DMUs or EMUs entered service.

Steam Happenings

Once again, the winter season played havoc with the diesel fleet, mainly due to train heating boiler problems, and steam was once again brought in to assist on a number of passenger turns.

Exmouth Junction shed, which on Christmas day 1963 housed 64 engines, was expected to lose most of its allocation by the year end.

With the demise of the A4s on the Eastern and North Eastern Regions it might have been expected that the class would no longer appear south of Newcastle, but the Scottish Region wished to continue having the class repaired, this work being carried out at Darlington works where 60004 was present in February. Conversely, many LMS types requiring overhaul were now being sent to Cowlairs works for attention. On returning south of the border these engines could be easily identified as the Scottish works was unique

Members of the Hall class became regular Saturday visitors to Nottingham Victoria in 1964 with 6998 Burton Agnes Hall *being recorded on August 11. A J Clarke/Colour-Rail.com*

Britain's Railways in the 1960s 39

Standard 4MT 75002 heads towards Talerddig summit whilst on Cambrian duties. The engine also received attention at Eastleigh works during the year. Colour-Rail.com

introduced, 9Fs were mainly confined to the Western and Eastern Regions along with the East Midlands but with the onset of dieselisation, particularly those based in the East Midlands, started to gravitate northwest. Thus, their arrival in Carlisle for allocation to Kingmoor was noteworthy and took the class regularly into Scotland for the first time. Football excursions in Scotland were not reported very often, no doubt because they often used commonly seen motive power. However, the Scottish Cup final on April 25 involved Glasgow Rangers and Dundee United and attracted nine specials from Dundee, most being hauled by V2s. Rangers won the tie 3-1.

The early part of the year had seen the Western Region condemn a 9F, 92223, and Standard 5MTs 73050/94. Whilst some condemned engines were beyond redemption, others appeared to have plenty of life left in them and these were reinstated by the Midland Region and returned to traffic. However, by the year end large numbers of BR Standards had been withdrawn and the only two steam classes from any origin that remained unscathed were the Britannias and the 77XXX Standards. May saw the demise of the long serving M7 0-4-4Ts on the Southern with their remaining duties going to either Ivatt 2MTs or Standard Class 4s.

The beginning of the end for steam on the Salisbury to Exeter route was signalled by the start of training on Warships at Exmouth Junction on June 1, 1964 and from the end of the summer timetable the Atlantic Coast Express was diesel worked, as were a number of other services. The first condemnation of a Merchant Navy was recorded and at the other end of the country time was almost up for both the J72s and V3s working around Newcastle, these being the last tank classes working on the Eastern and North Eastern Regions. The end of the summer timetable saw many withdrawals, perhaps the most notable of which was the elimination of the Duchesses.

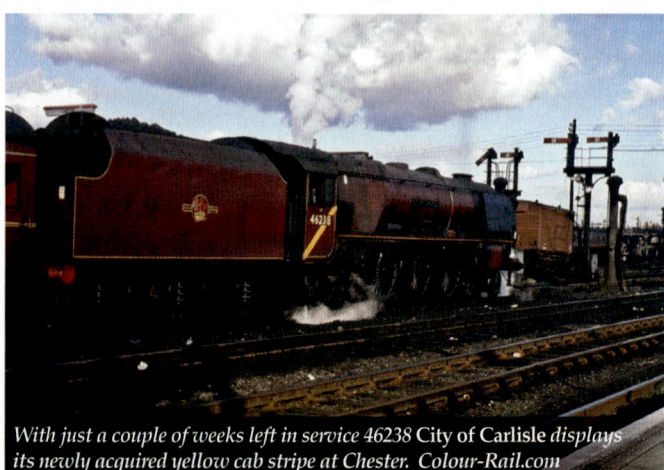

Their movements in the last few months were frequently recorded as had been those of the A4s a year previously. Many Jubilees also succumbed leaving the Britannias as the main express class on the Midland Region. Another class watched by enthusiasts were the Somerset and Dorset 7Fs and they

With just a couple of weeks left in service 46238 City of Carlisle displays its newly acquired yellow cab stripe at Chester. Colour-Rail.com

were also eliminated from stock when 53807 was condemned. Steam also had its last fling at Wadebridge with the 1366 class panniers replaced by 204hp diesels.

Steam withdrawals far exceeded the number of new locomotives delivered, partly achieved by the condemnation of many stored engines, but also due to the contraction of work. The total

Rowsley shed closed during 1964. In slightly better times – August 1961 - two 4Fs and a Jinty rest outside. Colour-Rail.com

reduced by 2,077 during the year. Despite this the areas in which steam could be seen had not contracted that much although the East Coast mainline south of Grantham and former GWR routes west of Taunton were of note. Generally, steam was just spread more thinly than before but areas such as North Wales, the northwest generally and pockets of activity in the northeast were where steam work still exceeded diesel appearances.

Infrastructure and Rolling Stock.

The year saw the general introduction of the use of concrete sleepers in combination with that of welded rails. They were said to have a life expectancy double that of wooden ones.

What was said to be the first diesel depot on the network, Devons Road in North London, closed on February 10 whilst Wolverhampton Stafford Road works out shopped its last engine on February 11. The demolition of the first of four roundhouses at Old Oak Common shed took place early in the year. Many of the smaller sheds across the country were being shut, in some places because of the complete elimination of steam, but in others the dwindling allocation was just moved to another depot nearby. Rowsley was an example with its remaining steam engines reallocated to Derby.

Duties included providing engines for the steeply graded Cromford and High Peak line whilst another depot to close was Polmont with duties transferred to Grangemouth.

The long running West Coast electrification project continued during 1964 with the section from Lichfield to Nuneaton energised from January 3 with through running implemented to there on March 2 and to Rugby from June 15. However, work to rebuild Wolverhampton High Level only started in February whilst that at New Street commenced in April. As construction progressed there was a comment about the increasing gloom at platform level at the latter as the vast overhead concrete structure grew, a problem not overcome to this day. It was costed at £2.5m with completion due at the end of 1966, at which time Snow Hill and the line to Wolverhampton from there would close. The overhead between Tring and Watford was energised on September 1 with electric working as far as Rugby planned for November 30. Rugby signal box went live in September replacing 22 others in the area.

Phase three of the opening of Healey Mills yard took place on March 2, 1964. However, the decline in wagon load freight saw the demise of the large marshalling yard at Westerleigh near Bristol.

Perhaps a foretaste of the modern large station was an initiative in Huddersfield, where a development company discussed plans with the local council for a commercial development at the station with shops, a bus terminal and a heliport included in the proposal.

BR approached the Ministry of Transport to see if lines such as that through central Wales could be operated under Light Railway regulations. Proposals included tickets issued by the guard, unstaffed stations, and open or automatic level crossings. It was claimed that losses could be reduced from £176,000 to £30,000 per year.

The hard winter of 1962/3 prompted a review of 'winter defences' with the result that nearly 2,000 new point heaters were to be installed and 15 new snow ploughs ordered. What could not be prepared for was flooding due to heavy rain, but on December 12 central and north Wales were hit with many lines damaged and some closed. As some of the lines breached were scheduled for closure anyway this proved to be the last day of use.

Services

On the central division of the Southern Region a new freight timetable came into force on January 6 with through services such as Brighton to Willesden and Three Bridges to Brent. Almost all freight services within the division were to be handled by diesel or electric power. On the same date Oxted line passenger services were revised giving improved journey times but also bringing an appreciable reduction in mileage run with push-pull trains in the area eliminated.

Another Southern change involved the through Brighton-Plymouth service which was to be decelerated due to it running via Portsmouth, and this was seen as the nail in the coffin of cross country trains to Brighton, which had already lost through trains to Bournemouth and Bristol. North of the Thames 'The Night Limited' was a new first class sleeper service between Euston and Glasgow on which the Nightcap Bar would be open until 1am.

Proposals were announced for diesel-hauled services between ➤

The West Coast scheme edged its way towards London and through running to Nuneaton had started in March. E3064 is in action there on August 31. K Fairey/Colour-Rail.com

Britain's Railways in the 1960s — 41

Waterloo and Exeter which had a 'more logical pattern of stops' between Salisbury and Exeter. What was not said was that this would slow down the service making it less attractive for through passengers. In Devon and Cornwall, the Southern route saw freight services diverted to run via GW lines and passenger trains were observed to be lightly loaded.

The pace of closures ramped up with 20 notices being implemented in the first quarter of the year and a further 38 approved by the minister of transport. One of the few rejections was that of the Central Wales line but casualties included both the Ringwood and Fordingbridge lines.

Whilst most lines for closure were rural in nature and of reasonable length, the proposed shutting of the branch between Stourbridge Junction and the Town station, at less than a mile in length, also brought out protestors in large numbers. Edinburgh-Berwick local services were a casualty on May 2. Some services saw little opposition or interest in their withdrawal, one such being Darvel to Ardrossan, where just one carriage sufficed even on closure day. Such was the pace of closures that in Q2 of the year more than 60 lines lost passenger, freight or both services, although a few them saw just the closure of intermediate stations. It was a rare thing for proposals to be rejected but the lines north of Inverness to Wick, Thurso, and Kyle of Lochalsh were refused for closure. Another round of closures occurred in the autumn including that of Blackpool Central. However, the minister refused to sanction closure of the Middlesbrough to Whitby route via Battersby or Bradford & Leeds to Skipton via Ilkley.

Despite rejections, BR frequently had another attempt at removing services. One example being the Gloucester-Chalford services, saved in 1962, which were discontinued from October 31, 1964. Indeed, the list of closures for the second half of 1964 exceeded 100 entries whilst that for refusals totalled six including S&C stopping services, Llandudno-Blaenau Ffestiniog and Richmond-Darlington.

Following the running of experimental services in 1963, cars built by Ford were to be carried by three trains per week from Dagenham and two per week from Halewood to Bathgate for distribution within Scotland. Another block car train began operation from Fawley to Hethersett. At the same time fish train services were under the spotlight as traffic had fallen by 55% in a decade. As well as the unremunerative single van consignments, 25 block trains were operating which BR wished to reduce to nine. The average load per train was only 35 tons of fish and just two tons per van.

The further reduction in inter-regional services to the Sussex coast on summer Saturdays saw only trains from Walsall, Wolverhampton, and Manchester and all terminated at Eastbourne, rather than running through to Bexhill or Hastings.

Hindsight gives an interesting perspective on some of the line closure proposals and how they have played out. The withdrawal of services from stations between Leamington and Coventry were deemed to cause no hardship. The re-instatement of Kenilworth station in recent years shows how

Two carriages and a van sufficed at Ringwood suggesting that the closure decision was justified. Standard 4MT 76025 officiates. R Patterson/Colour-Rail.com

The line from Middlesbrough to Whitby survived to become the only rail link to the now popular Yorkshire resort. Even this route required a reversal at Battersby where this MCW DMU was photographed. Colour-Rail.com

42   *Britain's Railways in the 1960s*

A service lost in the year was that of through trains from the Midlands to Hastings. Two years earlier 5MT 44690 heads a Hastings-Manchester service at Denham Golf Club. M J Reade/Colour-Rail.com

Shorn of its nameplates it looked like the end might not be far off for Schools 30928 Stowe, but it was rescued and put on display by Lord Montague of Beaulieu. It is seen here at Stewarts Lane in 1963. Colour-Rail.com

things have changed. Stratford–on–Avon council were vociferous over plans to close the North Warwickshire line - a battle that was eventually won. A proposal to form a 'local transport board' in the West Midlands to fight closures and run the services surfaced, in fact a pre runner of the PTE which emerged a few years later. Even though two years earlier the Birmingham-Redditch route had seen increased services of 14 trains per day, it was now the subject of closure proposals. The start of the process to make the Waverley route a candidate for closure began in September with the withdrawal of the 'Waverley' and the only through service to St Pancras was a portion of the Thames Clyde Express. October 5 saw the closure of the Glasgow Central Low Level lines, apparently little used at the time and presenting a picture of 'undiluted horror' in respect of the lack of maintenance and soot laden walls.

Observations

A4 *Mallard*, having been repainted in Garter Blue and regaining its original number 4468, was moved to the Clapham Transport Museum whilst Schools class 30928 *Stowe* was purchased by Lord Montague for display at Beaulieu Abbey.

Station masters had long been associated with the running of nearly every staffed station in the country but as economy measures took hold station masters, (or area representatives as some were called), were being asked to look after up to five stations at a time.

Spotters in some parts of the country were seeing locomotives of classes that they had never expected to come across as convoys of withdrawn engines moved around with ex GW and SR locos in Norfolk whilst the East Midlands and all Southern engines heading for the South Wales scrap yards passed through Gloucester, as towing of dead engines was prohibited through the Severn Tunnel.

Perhaps a portent of things to come was seen on April 13 when the by now preserved 3442 *The Great Marquess* pulling three carriages was used for filming by the BBC on the Pickering-Whitby route. Looking for some 'excitement' much slipping was demanded by the producer on departure down the 1 in 49 from Goathland, this only being achieved after quantities of oil were poured on the rails. Another preserved engine in action was Jones Goods 103 which came south from Scotland to take part in filming near Bedford.

One of the most famous railtours of the era operated on May 9, this being the Castle finale on the Ian Allan special from Paddington-Plymouth and return. High speed running was planned throughout but all did not go to plan with the failure of 4079 *Pendennis Castle* on the outward leg but a record time was set on the return with 7029 *Clun Castle* between Plymouth and Bristol, which ultimately ensured the survival of this engine into preservation. However, for a business that was losing vast sums of money the cost of the preparation for this tour must have been substantial as all the engines undertook trials on Worcester-Paddington services and some were sent to Swindon works for repairs ahead of the run, with a total of eight engines being specially prepared for the duty.

With diesel engines being able to operate over longer distances than steam, some excursion traffic could provide a surprise. One such was the arrival of D1073 *Western Bulwark* at Brighton on a special from Stourbridge on Whit Sunday.

On the Western Region a new idea was to run 'Mystery Excursions' with, in theory, the participants having no idea where they might be going, although enthusiasts could have had some idea by seeing the motive power provided and the reporting number, which would be in the form 1X if going off the region or 1Z if within. In later years they became quite popular with in one case having to be run in three parts.

From mid-year certain classes of steam engine allocated to Midland Region sheds acquired a yellow diagonal stripe on the cabside to denote that they would not be allowed to work south of Crewe from September to ensure adequate clearance with the overhead live wire. These were applied erroneously to some engines including a Clan Pacific.

There is a well-known saying about statistics and on occasions they could certainly be interpreted in more than one way. In the case of a proposed bus replacement for trains from Lidlington to Bletchley around 10 miles away, BR quoted a travel time of well under an hour. What they did not say was that it required a change of buses and an overnight stay, thus extending the journey over two days.

An example of how not to run a railway was seen at Birmingham New Street. With its rebuilding, platform changes took place, one of which was that four trains from New Street to Worcester, which were designated as 'Western Region services', were moved to newly constructed Platform 12 which was deemed to be a Midland platform. The Western Region deleted them from its time table but the Midland did not add them to theirs!

Yellow cab stripes were applied in error to some engines. WD 90465 acquired one although it was unlikely ever to venture to Crewe as it was allocated to Ardsley at the time and is seen here near Basford. Colour-Rail.com

1965
OVERVIEW

We have now reached the halfway point in our journey through the 1960s. By 1965 it was still too early to assess if the results of the Beeching cuts would turn the tide for the railways but the financial results had certainly improved little so far, with the loss being reduced by just £13m to £120.9m from the 1963 to the 1964 closing figures. The decline in passenger numbers also continued and indeed would for another 15 years. Two main factors caused this in 1964, the continued growth in road transport and the closing of many lines with the resultant loss of admittedly low numbers of passengers. Motorway building and general road improvements were just ramping up so the attraction of the car and road haulage would only increase in the years to come. However, one sector that was growing was that of the car carrier train which had seen a 20% increase in usage in the previous 12 months.

Mention should also be made of the unchanging role of the railways in carrying much of the country's mail and newspaper traffic, with a new ten year deal being signed to transport the latter.

January 1, 1965 saw the motive power stock of 4,660 diesel and electric locomotives now almost in balance with steam power at 4,973 engines but with the large number of diesel and electric multiple units the balance was now firmly tipped in favour of the modern image. As part of that image, during the year British Rail was adopted as the formal title of the business. A second Beeching report was published in February with the title of 'The Development of the Major Railway Trunk Routes'. Freight was a primary focus of the document which strongly promoted the idea of block trains and the elimination of wagon load consignments. Possibly to help promote this strategy the BRB split the business into passenger and freight sectors.

Regional organisational changes also took place in Scotland where the three tier Headquarters, Division and District system saw the new Divisions of Glasgow, Edinburgh and Highland set up, with these being autonomous along with district management being removed, whilst headquarters staff would just deal with policy and planning for the region as a whole.

Two large computer projects were started at centres in Reading and Darlington. The former included keeping information about wagon stock and movements and was probably the forerunner of the TOPS system that was developed in the next few years. The year also saw the introduction of the 24 hour clock across the network.

The major project of the West Coast electrification rumbled on with electrification masts present at Euston by April. Freight trains were worked throughout to Willesden by electric power from the end of September and many trains were electrically hauled through to Euston by the year end.

The completion of electrification work on the section through to Birmingham and Wolverhampton was not expected until 1967. The Bournemouth electrification project also started to make progress with a suggestion that electric services as far as Basingstoke could start during the year. A less well documented electrification was that of the Manchester-Sheffield scheme which was extended by nearly 17 miles at its eastern end to reach Tinsley yard.

An interesting development for the time was an announcement that a deal had been agreed with Brush for that company to carry out maintenance work on the BR diesel fleet.

The year saw an almost 40% reduction in the steam fleet which stood at only 2,989 engines at the year-end whilst the modern traction loco fleet totalled 5,088 with 100 EMUs added to stock.

Modern Traction Scene

The year started with the Midland Region abolishing shed allocations for its mainline diesel fleet based on the old Midland Railway route and substituting an allocation by division, so becoming M14 for London, M15 for Leicester and M16 for Nottingham, but also used was ML for, in theory, those engines

The Sutton Coldfield car carrier was one of the longest established services. Royal Scot 46137 and the proud owner of an absent car pose for the camera. Colour-Rail.com

The scene at Euston station at the end of 1964 showed just how much work needed to be done to complete the project, with not an electrification mast in sight. And yet by the end of 1965 electric services were operational. Colour-Rail.com

44   Britain's Railways in the 1960s

1965

Accidents showed the vulnerability of some DMU stock to damage, resulting in 17 not surviving beyond 1965. This event at Royton was more severe than most but thankfully without loss of life. The train was empty and the driver somehow survived unscathed. Accident reports at the time recorded that the 6.5am Shaw to Royton four coach empty diesel unit lost control on a steeply falling gradient and collided with the buffer stop at around 40mph. The buffer and stone wall behind it were demolished and the leading coach dropped around three feet and continued across High Barn Street destroying two houses and badly damaging three others. Colour-Rail.com

A batch of 4 BIG and 4 CIG EMUs were delivered for the Southern Region. 7331 is seen at Hastings. John E Henderson/Colour-Rail.com

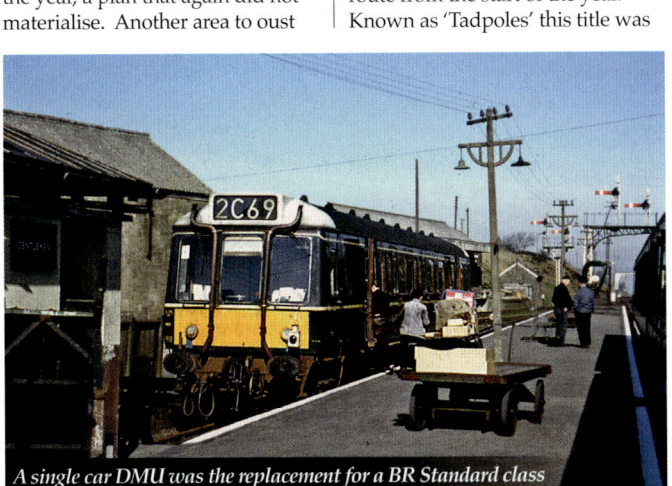

A single car DMU was the replacement for a BR Standard class 4MT and one or two coaches on some ex Southern routes in Cornwall as seen here at Halwill. R Patterson/Colour-Rail.com

employed on main line rather than local duties. Poor locomotive availability was a recurring theme with shortages reported, this being more of a problem in areas where steam engines could not be used as a replacement.

The use of diesel power for football specials increased and even for local events such as Aston Villa v Coventry DMUs rather than loco hauled stock were used. DMUs finally entered service on the Cambrian route in January with the steam worked Cambrian Coast Express and the daily mail train planned for diesel power during the year, a plan that again did not materialise. Another area to oust steam in favour of DMU operation were the former Southern lines in North Cornwall and to Bude. Yet more DMUs made surplus elsewhere were drafted in to work most passenger duties on the North Wales coast route except the through services to London.

The DMU fleet seemed particularly prone to accident and/or fire damage leading to withdrawal and by the start of the year no fewer than 17 cars had already been taken out of service from the 5XXXX number series.

'New' DEMU s took over steam duties on the Reading-Redhill route from the start of the year. Known as 'Tadpoles' this title was bestowed upon them due to the amalgamation of standard width stock with narrow bodied carriages from former Hastings line units.

An uprating of power provision was seen on Norwich-London services. Having started out with the 2,000hp EE Type 4s, these had been replaced by the 1,750hp Type 3. Now there was a big step up from January, as the 2,750hp Brush Type 4s took over these duties. This class rapidly spread its sphere of operation being noted from Aberdeen to the south coast. A typical long distance working was on the Milford Haven-Thornton oil trains with a Western Region engine as far as Carlisle, this being extended to its destination once crew training had taken place.

One of the most arduous steam duties had been the working of ore trains from Tyne Dock to Consett. Steam was initially replaced by English Electric Type 4s, but these were soon replaced in turn by pairs of D5XXX Type 2s.

The rebuilt North British Type 2 that had been at work in Scotland, D6123, appeared to be sufficiently successful to warrant the placing of an order to rebuild several other class members.

The first of a new batch of EMUs for the Southern Region appeared early in the year comprising 4 BIG 7031-48 and 4 CIG 7301-48.

At the same time, the first of a large batch of units, designated AM10 and painted in Rail blue, were delivered for the West Coast services from Birmingham southwards. Another order was placed for Type 4s from Brush for 20 further locomotives. The final deliveries of both the English Electric Type 3s and the D95XX diesel hydraulics took place towards the end of the year.

Inter-regional transfers of the small shunting types started to become more common. Some Eastern Region shunters had moved to the Western Region and then several Scottish examples in ➤

Britain's Railways in the 1960s 45

The newly delivered E31XX locomotives were used to run through to Willesden on parcels and freight duties before the wires into Euston were energised. Here E3115 is seen near Northchurch on October 20, 1965. Colour-Rail.com

the D27XX series were moved to Crewe and Wolverton to act as works shunters.

Locomotive naming had been restricted to the products of Swindon Works plus the early Peaks, EE Type 4s and Deltics, with the exception being the occasional later Peak which acquired a regimental name. Continuing to show its independence, on March 20 the Western Region named five Brush Type 4s after key GWR locomotives and personalities. In the next few weeks this extended to another dozen members of the class.

Electric power could be seen at a new maintenance depot built at Willesden with on March 29 E3032 present for staff training. The first of the new series of locos from E3101 upwards built at Doncaster were also noted at Crewe at this time and later at Rugby, again for training.

In a surprise move the Western Region carried out a trial with double headed EE Type 3s with a view to accelerating certain passenger services and these were used on a limited number of trains.

Tests got underway on the Southern on the operation of push pull trains that were needed for the Bournemouth electrification scheme. Trains going forward to Weymouth were planned to operate in that way and D6580 was the engine used initially on the test runs.

An emerging factor affecting locomotive availability was a lack of skilled staff to carry out the maintenance in some areas, this causing the cancellation of many freight services on the former Midland line out of London.

During the year 357 diesel locos were added to stock, these being Brush Type 4s D1646-81, D1702/3/5/6, D1773/92/5-1879/81-1925/63-83, EE Type 3s D6600-8, D6951-99, BR Type 2s D5299, D7519/21-65, D7624-40, and Type 1s D8587 and D8612-6 (Claytons) and D9517/22-55 hydraulics from Swindon. It should be noted that D1702-6 were fitted with an experimental 2,650hp engine and were all based at Shirebrook for evaluation. Also classed as new were D4500-2, these being paired up 350hp shunters in a master and slave format to work Tinsley yard. Seventy nine electric and electro diesels were also delivered as E3101-34/6, E3161-97, and E6007-13. One diesel class, the Brush Type 4s, was destined never to operate in its totality due to an accident at Shrewsbury which saw

One of the few surviving Q1 0-6-0s 33006 worked into nominal 'steam free' territory when employed on the Petworth goods. It is seen here resting at Guildford. Colour-Rail.com

46   *Britain's Railways in the 1960s*

The very last of more than 500 former LNWR 0-8-0s saw out their days based at Bescot shed. Here 48895, complete with yellow cab stripe is seen at work in the Walsall area shortly before its demise. Their replacements, the 4Fs lasted but three months or so before Standard 4MTs arrived in March 1965 to cover these turns. Colour-Rail.com

D1734 condemned.

Steam Happenings

In a speech made in Glasgow on January 19, 1965 the vice chairman of the BRB said that it was the intention to eliminate steam power in Scotland by the end of 1966 and across the whole system by the end of 1967. However, a result of the ban on certain classes of steam engine working south of Crewe was that to provide enough diesel power south thereof, steam workings northwards actually increased.

By the start of the year almost all cutting up of steam engines was put out to contract. That said some engines waited many months after condemnation before moving to a scrap yard and once there some were cut up within days whilst others survived for months. One yard that stood out was Woodhams at Barry. Engines had gone there for breaking since around 1961 and the early arrivals were reduced to scrap quite quickly but more recent arrivals were left in the large dock area whilst the company concentrated on the numerous wagons which they also processed.

As noted above, steam workings on the Reading-Redhill line ceased but steam 'popped up' at places where it had not been seen for some time such as the use of one of the few remaining Q1s 33006 on the Horsham-Petworth goods and at Lewes where steam was employed on a daily empty stock move.

Another place where steam made a brief comeback was on the Seaton and Lyme Regis branches were 14XX tanks replaced DMUs.

Swindon works ceased steam repair work in the first quarter of the year with 43003 being one of the last residents.

Previously, 1964 had seen the demise of the last engines of LNWR origin, being the G2 0-8-0s based at Bescot. These had been replaced by LMS 4Fs but within months these were also ousted, this time by Standard Class 4 2-6-0s 76036/42/7/86-8 which had all previously been at Saltley.

On the Western Region the goal had been set to be the first to rid itself of steam power, this to be achieved by the year end. However, it was still relatively widely spread from Slough in the east through to Llanelli in the west and from Exeter to Worcester as well as still being in almost sole command of the under threat Somerset & Dorset line.

With only the route to Bournemouth having regular steam power on expresses, enthusiast attention turned increasingly to the Glasgow-Aberdeen line where there were five duties that could/should have been worked by the A4s. Both A2 and A3 classes were still active as well and regularly seen at Dundee.

What might be viewed as the beginning of the end for steam was the withdrawal in June of the first Britannia 70007 *Coeur de Lion*. The migration of 9Fs previously referred to now saw a concentration of the class at Birkenhead, with the allocation expected to reach a total of 48 during the year. Out of 40 excursions recorded at Blackpool on Whit Monday, just five had diesel power with the majority worked by Stanier Black 5s, although 8F 48265 managed a day at the seaside with an excursion from Skipton.

The 16.15 Paddington-Banbury was the last timetabled steam worked duty from Paddington and June 11 saw the curtain come down on this when 7029 *Clun Castle* was rostered for the final turn. The following day it worked an excursion from Cheltenham to Weston-Super-Mare and got as far as Taunton for servicing.

As the last of class it was retained to work the final special steam train from Paddington, this taking place on November 27, running from there to Bristol and thence to Gloucester and Swindon, the trip concluding with a high speed run back to Paddington hauled by D6881/2.

All steam duties based on the Central division of the Southern Region ceased with the start of the summer timetable. Not so steam free were the sheds around Doncaster, Lincolnshire, and the ➤

7029 Clun Castle is seen departing from Paddington on June 11th with the final timetabled steam train from the terminus going through to Banbury. Colour-Rail.com

Britain's Railways in the 1960s 47

East Midlands that still had an allocation in excess of 320 engines at that time, whilst the North Eastern Region still had over 580 on its books with 470 in Scotland. The Scottish Region had for some time been reducing its steam stock every month despite not receiving any new locomotives, thus demonstrating how traffic continued to decline. The end for steam at the southern end of the West Coast mainline came with the start of the winter timetable when Willesden shed closed to steam, with Bletchley and Northampton already passed into history.

As the year-end approached the only steam sheds open on the Western Region were Severn Tunnel Junction, Gloucester, Worcester, Oxford, and those on the S&D. The final steam hauled push pull service in the country ceased operation in October when a DMU was substituted on the Seaton-Stamford line although its use was thought to be going to be temporary as the line was listed for closure. Illustrating the now famed north-south divide, observations found not a single mainline diesel noted in the first nine months of the year between Burnley and Colne.

Plans announced by the North Eastern Region for the elimination of steam stated that J27s and Q6 locos working in Co Durham and north of the Tyne would be the last engines in use and that replacement might not come until 1968, although numbers would reduce.

Steam withdrawals for the year totalled 1,985 with several classes rendered extinct. No classes survived intact as BR Standard 77010 was condemned, these 2-6-0s forming the last complete design.

Infrastructure and Rolling Stock

An example of how the progress of 'modernisation' brought forth great change was that of Oswestry, once the headquarters of the Cambrian Railway. The office buildings had long since closed and in recent times the shed and locomotive works suffered the same fate. The only trains that called from early 1965 were the occasional two car DMUs running to Gobowen and even that service was under threat.

Investment in the Central Wales line saw sections relayed using concrete sleepers but at the same time rationalisation took place at several locations with an extension of single line running. Four trains per day operated the through service.

Meldon Quarry near Okehampton had supplied ballast for the railways for many years and was in their ownership. However, it was announced that it would close by the end of the year with ballast being bought on the

An aerial view of a bustling Meldon Quarry. Plans to sell it to the private sector fell through. T Owen/Colour-Rail.com

Willesden shed, once bustling even as recently as February 1965, as seen here, ceased operations at the start of the winter timetable. T Owen/Colour-Rail.com

1965

commercial market. Unfortunately, like many of the modernisation plans it did not work out, the sale of the quarry to private enterprise fell through and Meldon survived to continue its ballast supply role.

With diesel power now well established almost across the country, it might be surprising that work was only just starting on providing diesel servicing provision at Frodingham, especially as Immingham shed was not far away. Fuelling facilities were also to be installed at Saltley with a capacity to service 100 locos per day and depot facilities were also to be built at Ebbw Junction. One new facility completed was a three-road shed at Old Oak Common.

The ongoing programme of shed closures saw Old Oak Common closed to steam with its remaining duties transferring to Southall whilst in the northwest, Bury and Gorton both shut along with the iconic Crewe North, but again to steam only. At the end of April, the Midland Region still had steam engines allocated to 70 depots.

Standard 4MT 80095 has just passed under Clapham Junction signal box which as can be seen spans many of the approach lines. The signal box collapsed in May 1965 bringing services in the area to a standstill. The report into the failure was published on October 25, five days after this picture was taken. Colour-Rail.com

A feature of lines across the regions for decades, except the Southern Region, was water troughs. Even though some diesel engines were fitted with pickup apparatus to fill the train heating boiler, with the demise of steam, the various troughs were abandoned with the year seeing most of those south of Crewe decommissioned.

A new signal box was brought into use at Reading which would eventually have control as far west as Didcot. Fortunately, major infrastructure failures were rare but one that made the headlines was the partial collapse of Clapham Junction signal box and, as it spanned many of the running lines, it brought the area to a standstill. Amazingly emergency repairs allowed most services to resume the following day.

With decreased traffic, plans were announced to close the old (dead end) station at Bristol Temple Meads and convert it to a car park.

An investment in the future was the announcement that a new design and development centre was to be built at Derby at a cost of £2.5m.

A trend that started in the 1960s was to build commercial developments on rafts over railway property, usually at major stations. One such scheme was at Ealing Broadway which included shops and a nine storey office block. Another building project was that of a new loco electrical test house at Doncaster works, said to be one of the most advanced in Europe. It could monitor the performance of two locomotives at once and was designed with considerable sound deadening capability using cork wall linings up to four inches thick. The test hall was separated from the control room by a concrete wall over two feet thick.

Services

Marketed as an airport service, some West of England expresses started to call at Slough with a road coach provided to take passengers to 'London Airport,' the name Heathrow having not yet been adopted.

The on-off dieselisation of Worcester-Paddington services had seen Hymeks employed on most duties from the 1964 winter timetable but it was announced that from June 14 Brush Type 4s would take over and journey times would be cut by up to 25 minutes.

As well as the large closure programme for passenger services, there was a rapid decline in the number of locations that handled freight traffic with 77 going in a four week period in the North Eastern Region alone. A few depots in London also closed with the plan being to have just six in due course. On the other side of the coin two more large oil ➤

The dieselisation of Paddington-Worcester services had been on the agenda since 1963 with Hymeks, Warships and Brush Type 4s all nominated to do the job, but it was into 1965 before steam was finally removed. Hymeks had been the most frequently mentioned candidates and here D7058 approaches Moreton in Marsh with a northbound service. Colour-Rail.com

Britain's Railways in the 1960s

companies signed long term deals to move products in block trains.

The battle to save the Great Central route was gradually being lost with nearly all freight services withdrawn or re-routed from June, leaving just seven long distance but slow passenger trains operating. The Somerset & Dorset line was likewise seeing out the last rites with its sparse service of stopping trains. Rerouted GC trains and the closure of Leamington and Didcot sheds however were bringing new life to Banbury where the shed had to provide power for 43 goods trains each weekday with all but two of them steam worked.

Closures continued apace through the first half of the year, with the majority of passenger service losses being those of local trains, but there were several major losses of passenger routes such as Ruabon to Barmouth, Walsall-Rugeley, Torrington-Halwill, Aberystwyth-Carmarthen, Bishop Auckland to Crook, Whitby-Scarborough and Malton, Dumfries-Kirkcudbright and Fraserburgh to St Combs.

Again, refusals were few but Stourbridge to Stourbridge Junction was one, along with Firsby to Skegness and Peterborough to Grimsby Town. An equally long list applied to the second half of the year which included the likes of Lakeside-Ulverston, Calne-Chippenham, the Lyme Regis branch, Bournemouth West, York to Beverley, Dumfries-Stranraer, the Killin branch and Aviemore to Elgin. Notable refusals were Broad Street-Richmond, the Redditch branch (reduced to just four trains per day), and local services between Fort William and Mallaig.

A new power station was built as Ferrybridge C and was planned to be served by Merry go Round coal trains from the outset which involved the building of a new 1,170 yard double track connection from the L&Y Goole Wakefield-Goole line.

As the road building programme gathered pace, large quantities of aggregates were moved by rail with 120,000 tons of stone from Wrexham to Dunton Green for the Sevenoaks bypass being but one example. Another large contract was that signed with Tartan Arrow which was to move all their goods on the Glasgow-London route for 20 years in block trains.

A new closure plot emerged in Sheffield with the advent of the winter timetable when 50% of the services that ran from and to

The windswept St Combs station with a train for Fraserburgh had reached the end of its time serving the local community and the Cravens DMU would have to be found employment elsewhere. Colour-Rail.com

*Manor 7819 **Hinton Manor** (well that is what it was thought to be as it had neither name nor numberplates), instead of being based at the shed at Aberystwyth, following the closure of the shed, now had to run light from Machynlleth to take up its duties. T Owen/Colour-Rail.com*

50   Britain's Railways in the 1960s

Victoria station were diverted to serve Midland instead, most of those remaining being the Trans Pennine electrics to Manchester via Woodhead.

Dr Beeching formally opened the new facility at Tinsley on October 29, built at a cost of £10m. It had nearly 60 miles of track and could sort 4,000 wagons per day using 23,000 speed detectors and 13,000 accelerate/retard units, all controlled by tape fed computer systems and replacing nine local yards.

Observations

Possibly one of the most observed trains of all time ran on January 30, 1965 when Battle of Britain 34051 *Winston Churchill* hauled the wartime Prime Minister's funeral train from London to Bladon in Oxfordshire with crowds filling stations and standing on the lineside throughout the route.

A very unlikely candidate for works attention at Eastleigh was Jubilee 45699 *Galatea* which duly arrived hauling an 8F, also for attention.

The XP64 prototype train moved from use on the Eastern Region to the Midland in January and then to the Western on March 1. The blue-painted Brush Type 4 D1733 did not always work with the XP64 stock, being noted on a freight at Basingstoke in April. Through diesel workings on freight services could see the appearance of unexpected diesel classes outside of their normal area of operation. One train to provide these was a Cardiff-Corby working that was powered by Hymeks and Westerns as well as Brush Type 4s.

No fewer than 25 football excursions ran from Liverpool to London for the FA Cup final and the return northwest would have been a happy one as Liverpool won the trophy for the first time in their history, beating Leeds United 2-1. All the football specials were electrically worked to Rugby with diesel traction going forward.

Some so called economies seemed to make little sense. One such was the closure of Aberystwyth as a shed. With crews then having to sign on at Machynlleth, at least three engines had to run light from there to Aberystwyth daily to take up their duties. A bit of colour was added to services around Bristol following the transfer of several carriages carrying Southern green livery to blend with the maroon and still in use chocolate and cream stock.

Summer Saturday cross country services from Wolverhampton to the West Country were providing almost the only steam activity at Bristol but brought regular workings by Britannias, a class that had never been particularly common in the area. Conversely, trains from the Eastern and North Eastern Regions through to Bristol employed a string of Tinsley based Brush type 4s with those fresh from the builder being easily distinguished from a distance by their ultra-clean roof louvres.

On occasions locomotives being taken for scrapping at Barry were worked throughout by a Southern based engine with Battle of Britain class 34051 noted on several occasions before returning light engine on each occasion.

The image portrayed of the railways in many areas was not one that would attract passengers with unmanned and unkempt stations along with overgrown deserted yards covered in weeds. With so many services withdrawn the demolition teams could not keep up with the removal of buildings and track.

Much of the steam locomotive fleet away from the northwest of England likewise presented a picture of filth and poor maintenance, with ex-GWR engines coming off the worst with number plates removed and crude hand-painted numbers substituted. What turned out to be the very last bank holiday excursion from Bath to Bournemouth via S&D metals ran on August 30, 1965 with 73001 in charge. Despite the delivery of new locomotives slowing down, the pace of steam withdrawals did not, once again reflecting the contraction of duties overall with for instance the Scottish Region taking 29 engines out of stock in September whilst receiving just three new engines, the first of nine Brush Type 4s to join its fleet. However, the first of the rebuilt D61XX like D6123 did enter traffic. Despite the ongoing rundown of the Scottish fleet, steam returned on the Glasgow-Gourock route with nine trains a day converted from DMU operation due to poor availability of the units.

Around this time Rail Blue was adopted as the standard livery, and whilst it was yet to appear on a locomotive other than D1733, coaching stock repaints were in blue and grey for passenger carrying stock but all-over blue on much of the parcels stock.

A derailment and subsequent collision occurred near Bridgend on December 19, 1965 following a landslip. The incident resulted in both the locomotives involved, Class 47 D1671 and D6983, being condemned and sold for scrap although that would not happen until 1966.

*A once proud 70053, formerly named **Moray Firth** presented an image of utter filth to onlookers at Bristol Temple Meads as it returned holiday makers from the West Country to the Black Country on August 21, 1965. P Chancellor/Colour-Rail.com*

Closed just two years previously, Congresbury on the former Cheddar Valley line, like many other closed stations, was gradually returning to nature. J R Newman/Colour-Rail.com

1966
OVERVIEW

The year opened with the by now traditional senior management staff changes. This included the appointment of a chief officer (special duties), whose role was to assist the other board members in the implementation of the modernisation plan. Some regional boundary changes took place including the shed at Colwick becoming part of the Midland Region, which immediately saw a mass transfer of LMS types to replace the incumbent Eastern machines.

The annual financial results issued in mid-1966 showed that the deficit had increased again for 1965 to £132m although the operating deficit decreased for a second year. A 23% reduction in the number of staff was recorded going down to 365,000. The number of freight depots fell from 2,833 to 1,934 and while freight receipts fell by £8m, passenger receipts were up by £6m.

The boom and bust UK economy took a downturn in 1966 leading to an announcement that further operational economies were to be sought with a targeted reduction of 6% in train miles.

With steam locomotive numbers now reduced to below 3,000, the target for the elimination of steam by the end of 1967 looked possible but with only around 150 locomotives on order, plus the Bournemouth electrification plans, there was certainly some challenging arithmetic to be done. However, the Western Region did go all diesel from January 4 except for the S&D lines.

The Bournemouth electrification scheme was the major project for the year.

Works still carrying out steam repairs at the start of the year were Inverurie, Glasgow, Darlington, Crewe, and Eastleigh but Darlington out shopped its last steam engine, 70004, in January.

A notable arrival was D8128, the first of an order for 100 English Electric Type 1s. These proved to be among the last engines ordered to complete the elimination of steam and were remarkable in as much as they were ordered instead of more Claytons, which were supposed to be the Type 1 of the future. Later in the year a further order for 50 Type 4 locos was placed based on the prototype DP2, which had been running on the network for some time. Although delivery was stated to be in 1967, by the time the last machines arrived steam was already dead. They were intended for use between Crewe and Glasgow.

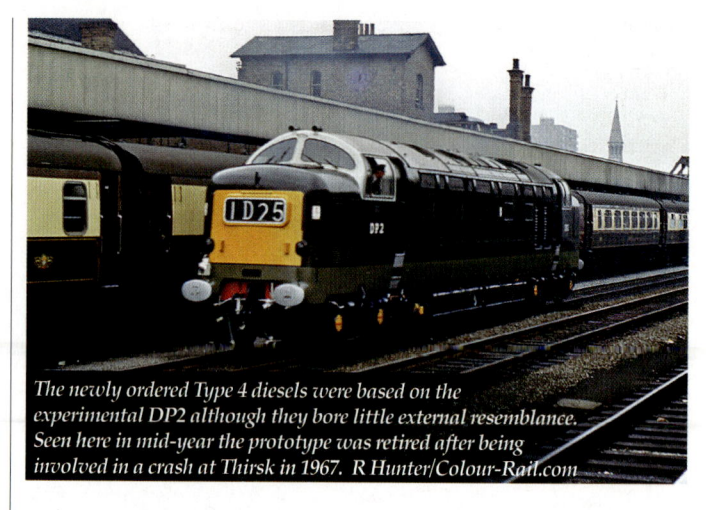

The year also saw the first deliveries of the Mk 2 carriage, its design having been derived from that used in the experimental XP64 set, with the first examples going to the Midland Region. New freight stock also came into service in the shape of oil tank cars which weighed in at 90t when fully loaded and were for use by Shell and BP. They could run at a maximum speed of 60mph. Another 'fleet' that was to be expanded was that of British Transport Police dogs up from 47 to 75.

In what proved to be an extremely over optimistic requirement, the BRB apparently issued an instruction that there were to be no steam passenger train workings after September 3 except on the Southern Region, nearly two years before that actually came to pass.

Overall, 1966 saw the withdrawal of 1,298 steam engines, or just over 30% of the total at the end of 1965, with the addition of just 213 diesel and electric locomotives. There was actually a fall in the number of DMU cars in service although only by 28 and there was a small increase in EMU stock.

Modern Traction Scene
A notable service withdrawal from January 3 was that of the EMU-worked trains from Lancaster to Morecambe, with the stock being condemned.

The DMUs of the time did not appear to have a strong enthusiast following but note was taken of a Lincoln-based two car unit coupled to a Trans Pennine set and running on Hull-Liverpool services.

For diesels to take over duties on the Burry Port-Gwendraeth route, which had a restricted loading gauge, D2141-6 received a modified cab roof profile along with a reduced height chimney.

A line seeing little variety of haulage, Oxford-Worcester, was

The newly ordered Type 4 diesels were based on the experimental DP2 although they bore little external resemblance. Seen here in mid-year the prototype was retired after being involved in a crash at Thirsk in 1967. R Hunter/Colour-Rail.com

Britannia 70004 was the last steam engine to be out-shopped from Darlington works. Its better than average condition meant that it was a prime choice for railtour duty and on August 14, 1965 it worked one from Westbury on to the Southern Region. R K Greenhalgh/Colour-Rail.com

1966

M29023M heads a three car unit at Lancaster Green Ayre. The service was the first casualty of the year with the stock condemned. Colour-Rail.com

enlivened in January using D6943 as a banker at Honeybourne and D6525 arriving with a consignment of turnips at Evesham.

Crewe based Brush Type 4s started to work through to Bournemouth on the Pines Express and the engine that arrived on a Saturday had a return run to Waterloo on a Sunday.

A further stage of electric working to be implemented on the West Coast scheme saw trains so hauled through from Wolverhampton to Stafford on April 18. The completion of wiring took place at Birmingham New Street on October 11 and was energised on October 31. Full electric working started on December 6, 1966.

A mass transfer of North Eastern DMUs to Scotland enabled the Gourock services, that had reverted to steam power some months earlier, to again be diesel worked from mid-April. As a result of these arrivals a grand reallocation of Scottish DMUs ensued with 257 cars involved, the net result of which was that a total of 23 extra cars were allocated to Dundee, Hamilton and Ayr at the expense of Inverurie, Corkerhill and Leith. A concentrated effort to remove all steam from the Waverley route had also been made and only a couple of local freights remained booked for steam power from the end of January.

Some problems only emerge over time and one such was the failure of engine sumps on Brush Type 4s due to metal fatigue. The rectification programme involved sending engines at the rate of two per week to the Sulzer works at Barrow whilst others were to be dealt with at BR workshops.

The allocation scheme for main line diesels on the Midland Region changed again in April with the extension of the previous divisional codes to the West Coast route with D01 created for London, D02 for Birmingham and D05 for Stoke.

With (in particular) the Brush Type 4s now penetrating almost the full length of the country, through workings of locomotives were becoming much more prevalent and thus less worthy of recording by the railway press of the day. Many of these were by now part of everyday operation and, for instance, summer Saturday services from the North East of England to the southwest taking Tinsley and Gateshead engines through to the likes of Paignton and Plymouth.

An area that had to date seen few diesel locomotives was the Cambrian from Shrewsbury to Aberystwyth but on June 25, 1966 EE Type 3 D6984 arrived and crew training was undertaken with it working the Cambrian Coast Express regularly.

No sooner had the Western Region completed the removal of steam power than it was able to squeeze more locomotives out of the system with, for example, in June 12 each of Brush Type 4s and EE Type 3s being transferred to the Midland and North Eastern Regions respectively with many more following in due course.

Merry go Round (MGR) coal trains were introduced in 1966 and they were generally discharged 'on the move' at very slow speed. To assist in this process several diesels were fitted with slow speed control apparatus and D5300/3 were so noted in Scotland in July.

The XP64 train with D1733, had been launched back in 1964 and whilst coaching stock had since appeared in blue and grey, ➤

Work was completed on the rebuilding of Euston station with the modern lines of the frontage being seen here. T Owen/Colour-Rail.com

Britain's Railways in the 1960s 53

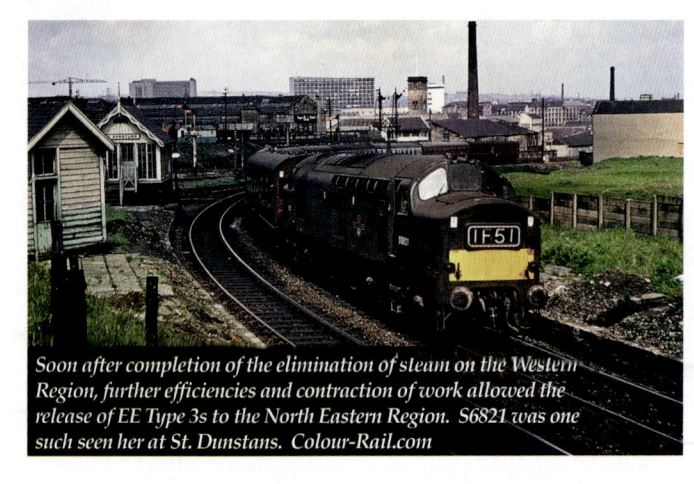

Soon after completion of the elimination of steam on the Western Region, further efficiencies and contraction of work allowed the release of EE Type 3s to the North Eastern Region. S6821 was one such seen her at St. Dunstans. Colour-Rail.com

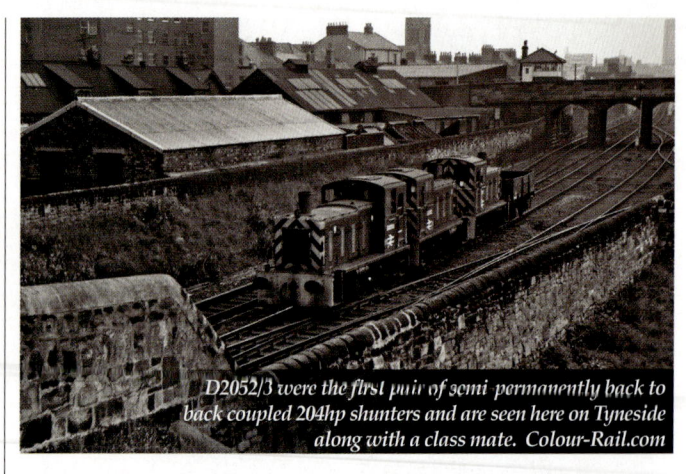

D2052/3 were the first pair of semi-permanently back to back coupled 204hp shunters and are seen here on Tyneside along with a class mate. Colour-Rail.com

locomotives other than electrics had continued to come out in green, but on August 10 D1030 was noted at Exeter painted blue and D3274 emerged from Eastleigh painted similarly a few weeks later.

Other than EMUs used on the West Coast route and those at Glasgow, blue had not been applied to any electric units but Eastern units 004, 214 and 404 emerged so painted in July. Indeed, blue would be the standard colour from now on, although the number of variances in the minutiae of its application saw many livery differences emerge. Interestingly, the first Warship to gain the blue livery soon had a dark maroon skirt.

The last region to receive an allocation of Brush Type 4s was the Southern where D1921-6 arrived. Being the only diesels fitted with steam heating they were thus able to work winter passenger services on the Bournemouth route.

D2052/3, a pair of 204hp shunters, were observed semi permanently coupled at York to give a haulage capability equal to a Type 1 locomotive for evaluation ahead of a possible fleet of 20 such pairs.

New diesel locomotive deliveries comprised only D1100-7, D1704, D1880, D1926-56/84-99, D7566/7/98-7623, D7641-66 and D8128-84, Electrics E314160/98/9 E3200 and Electro Diesels E6014-48. A total of 18 diesels were condemned.

Steam Happenings
As noted previously, January 3, 1966 saw the final day of steam operation on the Western Region, this being achieved without any additional diesel engines being added to the fleet. The only marking of the event was the use of a very bulled up 6998 on a passenger turn from Oxford to Banbury.

Ex-GW types continued to be active at sheds then under control of the Midland Region. It did not however bring an end to steam workings on the region as the York-Bournemouth service employed both Stanier 5MTs from Banbury and Bournemouth based Southern and Standard types on through workings via Didcot and Reading West, as well as initially frequent arrivals at Gloucester of freight trains from the Birmingham area. The Banbury engine often turned out to be a 5MT from elsewhere with Manchester and North Wales based engines being noted amongst others. However, the Western Region's steam free ambition was thwarted by the last minute retention of the S&D route due to problems with replacement buses. Minimal services were provided for a further two months, the final rites being performed by two special trains on March 6.

For a brief period in 1965 Britannias had taken over many passenger duties on the Great Central line but with these being transferred away Stanier 5MTs would dominate until closure.

The Scottish Region crept towards the elimination of steam power with the full dieselisation of Dundee-Glasgow trains whilst on the Eastern the end of March saw Doncaster as the only shed with an

Possibly the first BR 350 hp diesel shunter to appear in blue livery was D3274 seen here at Eastleigh. Colour-Rail.com

1966

The very last steam hauled passenger service under Western Region auspices saw Hall 6998, complete with wooden nameplates, work from Oxford to Banbury on January 3rd. R Denison/Colour-Rail.com

active steam allocation, this being of just 36 engines, and the end came there just a few days later. However, visitors had included things not often seen in previous years such as a St Margarets allocated V2 and a Banbury based 9F.

Darlington shed closed at the end of March and along with it the steam pilot duty which had found gainful employment for the last two A1s.

Ayrshire was a pocket of steam activity, but the fleet had been run down as diesels had been promised in the spring. These failed to materialise and a few of the steam engines were sent to Cowlairs works for light repair to keep the services running.

An oasis of regular steam passenger work was the Shrewsbury-Birkenhead leg of the through trains from Paddington, usually worked by a Class 5 loco although some trains on the Wirral attracted a Crab or 4MT tank.

Meanwhile the 'steam free' border lines gradually continued their progress north with Derby and Coventry becoming boundaries in mid-year.

Because dual heated stock was not available, one long-standing winter steam duty remained along the south coast, this being the Brighton-Plymouth service, which in four months of operation had 30 different Bulleid Pacifics, 12 Standard 5MTs and 75068 as power to Salisbury.

Even on the southwestern division of the Southern the wind of change was blowing with a Saturday observation at Worting Junction, showing that out of 80 trains, 43 were diesel worked.

A feature of several railtours in recent years, especially north of the border, were the four 'preserved' locomotives from the various constituent companies. Their operational careers came to an end in June when they were all moved into the new transport museum at Coplawhill in Glasgow where they were joined by an ex Glasgow and South Western tank.

The last three Leeds Holbeck allocated Jubilees, 45593 45675/97, were booked to work summer Saturday services over the Settle & Carlisle route and attracted much attention from enthusiasts and steam was also turned out for many similar duties over Shap too.

When steam was the norm, some sheds used to employ one of the allocation on a temporary basis as a stationary boiler to provide steam for various purposes. Another job was the use of an engine to heat ➤

A1 60140 Balmoral stands at the south end of Darlington shed as stand by engine, ready to replace any ailing express engine. An engine had stood there day in and day out for many years, but the duty came to an end with the closure of the shed. Colour-Rail.com

A4 60019 Bittern brought down the curtain on steam operation of the Glasgow-Aberdeen expresses and is seen here near Gleneagles in April 1966. M Chapman/Colour-Rail.com

Britain's Railways in the 1960s

55

Old meets new at Normanton as 9F 92047 rolls through Normanton with an oil train. The tanks are relatively modern and yet within a couple of years designs carried on bogies instead of four wheels, with a weight of 100t, would become the big new thing. P J Fitton/Colour-Rail.com

stock ahead of departure time. Now that steam had disappeared from operational duties at many locations, some engines were being retained specifically to cover these duties in the heart of otherwise diesel territory.

The ending of the summer timetable and its Saturday extras saw many lines return to essentially diesel only operation on passenger duties. One casualty was the Glasgow-Aberdeen service where A4 60019 brought down the final curtain.

Conversely, steam usage increased on the Cambrian lines with the Cambrian Coast Express being a regular duty. However, this did not last long with BR Type 2 diesels arriving for the next bout of crew training. The Glasgow autumn holiday on September 23, when there was a mass exodus to Blackpool, saw 13 extras run via Shap, each one steam hauled throughout, including an engine change for each at Carlisle. Britannias predominated south of Carlisle and Stanier 5s north thereof.

Birkenhead shed had continued its gathering of BR 9Fs and had no fewer than 55 on its books in April.

Infrastructure and Rolling Stock

An early innovation in the year on the Scottish Region was the building of six lineside buildings using plastic panels for which a patent was obtained.

Stage 1 of the New Street resignalling scheme went live on January 8/9 with stage 2 due for completion in April. A new scheme was announced for re-signalling in the Swindon area at an estimated cost of £1.75m.

Rationalisation of track and signalling on the Minehead branch saw Minehead signal box closed with everything controlled from Dunster. At the other end of the scale the new signal box and re-signalling at Cardiff was completed at a cost of £3m, said to be the largest scheme on the region so far, replacing 33 boxes in total. A new scheme based on Gloucester was announced which would see 46 signal boxes closed.

A new station opened on April 1, this being Southampton Airport with the only public access being from the airport. The

Freightliner trains were introduced in 1966 and D1843 heads a service through Carlisle on August 10. Colour-Rail.com

1966

The locomotives that worked the Wisbech & Upwell tramway in Cambridgeshire were readily identifiable by the 'skirt' and cowcatchers required because they operated in unfenced areas. Custom does not appear to be heavy in this view at Upwell taken on November 3, 1962. Colour-Rail.com

Birmingham Curzon street site was to be developed as a freightliner terminal.

The building of a new oil terminal near Leeds was announced in November and was said to be the forerunner of several similar facilities. More than 400 oil trains per week were operating at this time.

The mechanisation of track maintenance together with the wide use of concrete sleepers were producing savings of £10m per year.

As hinted at back in 1963, proposals to single much of the line from Salisbury to Exeter were put forward with completion planned for 1967. Strangely, singling the line was said to be to enable faster services to be operated!

As the closure programme progressed a feature was the growing list of once major stations that were closed.

The use of computers in the industry was starting to accelerate and the first use of one for recording track defect information was reported and used the wonderful project name of 'North Eastern Electronic Peak Tracing Unit and Numerical Evaluator' otherwise known as Neptune!

New diesel shed facilities were still being built with a contract placed for one at Wigan Springs Branch in August, whilst that at Healy Mills was opened on June 27, 1966.

New fabrics for seating, carpets and curtains were trialled from the autumn in two specially equipped carriages with several combinations in each.

Services

Car carrying services continued to grow in popularity with a 50% increase in trade in the preceding year leading to five new routes being introduced for 1966. A new service was launched in July from Newton-le-Willows to Newton Abbot with a Western Lines Brush working throughout.

BR launched a container service under the brand name 'Freightliner' with containers painted silver with a red band. One of the early contracts was to move apples and pears from the London Docks to Glasgow. New services added in September were from Liverpool and Manchester to Glasgow. Refrigerated containers were to be built, initially to carry Scottish beef. The 10,000th container was carried on August 9, 1966, some nine months since the start of operations and the 20,000th carried in November.

The accelerated London-Hereford passenger service failed to attract customers with loadings noted as 'light' and there was talk of their withdrawal.

Despite the professed wish to reduce traffic that caused the poor utilisation of stock, the Western Region ran 120 holiday relief trains over the Easter break.

The first fruits of the West Coast electrification were seen when revised services were introduced on April 18 with ten trains to Manchester (via Crewe) and eight to Liverpool. The journey time was 2 hrs 35 minutes, a reduction of well over an hour compared with recent timings, giving an average speed of 74mph. Both cities were to have Pullman trains for which new stock was being delivered. The Manchester Pullman via the Midland route was withdrawn. However, Birmingham and services via Stoke were not expected to be upgraded for another 12 months. Services to Preston, Carlisle and Glasgow were also accelerated.

The Western, not to be outdone, had the 14.45 Paddington-Bristol train scheduled to run at an average speed of 78.4 mph to the first stop at Chippenham and 120 trains scheduled at over 60mph. On the Eastern they were also scheduling services at 70mph and introduced a new regular interval service pattern out of Kings Cross. The Flying Scotsman had its running time reduced to 5hrs 50 minutes. ▶

A railtour to mark the closure of the Great Central route was run on September 3, 1966 headed by 35030 Elder Dempster Lines and is seen here on arrival at Nottingham Victoria. Colour-Rail.com

Britain's Railways in the 1960s

Crewe South was still an important centre of steam activity as can be observed in this view taken on April 28, 1966. T Owen/Colour-Rail

A notable route closure in May was that of the Wisbech & Upwell tramway. With the line being in the main unfenced, the locomotives employed had always been fitted with 'cow catchers' and wheel valances and was thus were readily identifiable.

A train that attracted little attention was the Siege of Beattock, this being a Saturday-only single coach which ran from Shap summit calling 'as required' at the lineside cottages in which railway staff lived. The service took them to town in Beattock, returning at lunch time and delivering supplies of water and paraffin along the way. Unfortunately for the residents the service ceased on October 1, 1966.

Freightliner trains continued to be introduced with the latest being those to carry clay slurry from Cornwall to Longport and Sittingbourne. However, one service in decline was the carrying of horses by rail, with a rapid reduction in the number of horse boxes available for traffic.

The first rumblings on the future of the Waverley route emerged with BR targeting it for closure in 1967. However, The Waverley through train to St Pancras re-emerged for the summer season.

The pace of closures slowed somewhat in the first half of the year with more of a focus on Scottish lines such as Aberdeen to Ballater and Connell Ferry to Ballachulish. Many lines lost their local services such as Crewe-Chester, Exeter-Salisbury, and Reading–Westbury.

The end came for most of the Great Central route on September 3, an event marked by the running of a railtour headed for part of the time by Merchant Navy 35030, whilst attracting a lot less attention was the end of the 43 mile line between Taunton and Barnstaple.

That date also saw the end of most of the old Southern network in Devon and Cornwall. Other casualties in the second half of the year were Gobowen-Oswestry, Southampton Terminus, Saxmundham-Aldeburgh, Barrhead-Kilmarnock, and Glasgow Buchannan Street.

As part of the modernisation a National Freight Plan was gradually put in place. One result of this was a large reduction in freight traffic at the southern end of the Great Northern mainline.

Observations

A visit to Crewe South shed on January 2nd found 90 steam engines present.

These reflected the very much reduced variety of classes that would see out steam on the Midland Region with a preponderance of Stanier 5s and 8Fs, along with various BR Standard types including the Britannias. The remaining steam fleet appeared to wander more off the beaten track, but a rare occurrence was the use of Eastleigh's 76033 on a Southampton-York banana train, which it certainly worked as far as Sheffield. B1s started making regular appearances on the North Wales coast with 61017/9 and 61306 all noted in March.

Every move of the three remaining A2s allocated to Dundee was recorded in the railway press alongside those of the few remaining A4s, which were still employed on the Aberdeen services in the first few months of the year.

March was notable for the withdrawal of the second and final mainline diesels designed by the LMS, 10001. Also condemned was a former LMS 0-6-0 diesel shunter 12011 and the demise of this class would accelerate in the coming months.

A noted steam transfer was of the only 77XXX engine on the Midland, 77014, which went to the Southern Region where its use frequently attracted attention especially as a survivor until the end in 1967.

A leaflet issued by the Southern Region concerning the Bournemouth electrification advised the residents of Boscombe that the new service would give

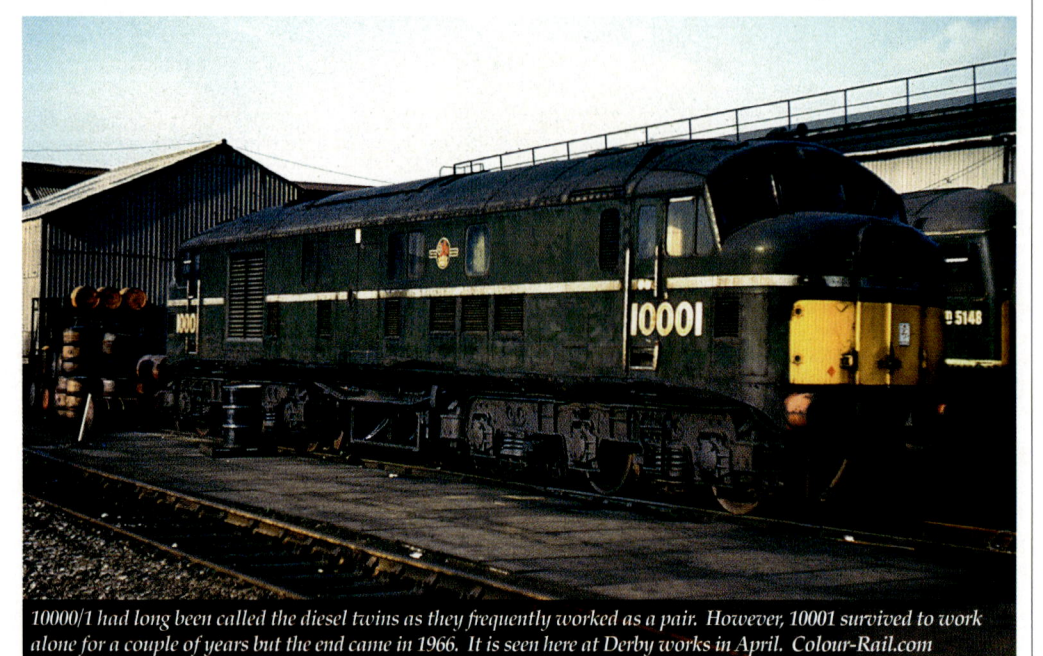

10000/1 had long been called the diesel twins as they frequently worked as a pair. However, 10001 survived to work alone for a couple of years but the end came in 1966. It is seen here at Derby works in April. Colour-Rail.com

58   Britain's Railways in the 1960s

The last steam engine to be repaired at Eastleigh Works, 34089 Battle of Britain 602 Squadron. Colour-Rail.com

them 28 trains per day to London, with a reduction of 35 minutes in the journey time. The only problem was that Boscombe station had closed several months earlier.

With the dieselisation of the Swanage branch in September the line to Lymington became the last steam worked branch in southern England. Despite many lines by this time not having any steam presence, BR was prepared to work engines through these areas on railtours and of special note were A4s 60019/24 from Scotland, the latter making it as far south as Weymouth, whilst Merchant Navy 35026 was noted at Nottingham. Later in the season 60532, 70004 and 60919 also came to the Southern although the latter failed and did not work its designated tour but once fixed the region made use of it before sending it home. Named *Lamport & Holt Line*, 35026 was again involved in October when it got as far north as Newcastle.

Football and rugby specials were still a major feature of operations and with diesel power available through locomotive workings became more common, with for instance the first appearance of an EE Type 3 at St Helens in the shape of Hull based D6741 on May 4, 1966. An interesting reallocation in June was that of Hunslet 0-6-0 shunter D2554 from the Eastern to the Southern Region, this engine then moving to the Isle of Wight to become the first diesel engine to work on the Island where it was used on permanent way duties.

Another unusual move was of NER departmental 52 to the Southern Region to work on the Bournemouth electrification project.

The final A1, 60145 was withdrawn by the North Eastern Region in June leaving the only English Pacifics in use being the Britannias and the Southern fleet. Another class to disappear was the LMS 4F 0-6-0 leaving just the Scottish and North Eastern Regions operating tender engines of that wheel arrangement, whilst November saw the withdrawal of the final standard gauge engine of Great Western origin, this officially being 0-6-0PT 9774 although subsequently the debate has raged about which was actually the last one in steam. A long standing feature on the Southern, that of fixed formation numbered coaching stock sets, started to be discontinued in mid-year, in part because many carriages were required for conversion for use in the Bournemouth line EMUs and trailer sets.

Despite much modernisation, the often overlooked stock of departmental carriages and wagons had seen little updating with several examples still being in use with over 60 years of service.

Steam repairs ceased at Cowlairs in September when 62059 departed leaving Crewe as the only works dealing with steam after 34089 was completed by Eastleigh on October 3. A Royal train duty brought two Westerns to Lewes on October 28, 1966 when D1054 worked the train to Merthyr with D1019 as standby.

Service stock had for some time provided two pockets of steam on the Southern, being in use at Ashford and Meldon, but the end came for both in 1966. ∎

D2554 became the first diesel locomotive to work on the Isle of Wight and was sent there only to carry out permanent way duties. It is seen here at Ryde during the electrification of the surviving part of the system. Colour-Rail.com

Britain's Railways in the 1960s

1967
OVERVIEW

In yet another organisational change the North Eastern Region was merged with the Eastern from January 1.

Time keeping had always been under scrutiny on the railways. In the autumn of 1966, the Western Region recorded just 40% of trains as being on time but by early in 1967 this had improved to 66% on time with another 20% being less than five minutes late. On the Eastern Region 172 trains averaged a lateness of 4.1 minutes compared with a pre-Christmas level of 7-8 minutes late. 86% of the services were operated by a Deltic or Brush Type 4.

The previously sanctioned design and development building at Derby was opened on March 31. Along with the 1964-built research laboratory the whole was renamed the Railway Technical Centre and had a staff of 12,000.

A new uniform was introduced for all catering car staff in the spring which included the Pullman services, although the uniform there was somewhat different.

An interesting development was the approval by the government of a request for the joint parcels operation that it ran with British Road Services, to be allowed to carry parcels by road for the whole of their journey.

A further batch of electric units were on order, this time to extend electric working around Glasgow, the new services starting on June 5, although not all the new units had arrived.

June 18 saw the running of the last electric unit on the Tyneside system with all services being DMU operated thereafter.

The first of a new variety of electro diesel appeared late in the year. These were in fact E5000 electrics now fitted with an additional 650hp diesel engine and were numbered from E6101 upwards.

An order was placed in the autumn for 400 Mk 2 carriages of which 137 were first class, the batch to be split between the Eastern and Western Regions.

The withdrawal of many diesel locomotives (see later) brought about an overall reduction of 219 engines in 1967. Despite this drop, 1,327 steam engines were also withdrawn in the year. DMUs suffered a similar fate and it was only the stock of EMU vehicles that saw an increase, by 220 carriages. At December 31 steam engines were only allocated to the Midland region.

Modern Traction Scene

Just over a year after the delivery of the final member of the class, the Western Region had sufficient surplus D95XX locomotives to allow 20 to be transferred to Hull to work in the docks. Another 11 were transferred in May. The clear out of the class on the Western saw the final examples leave Bristol after a reign of just two years.

Almost the last Brush Type 4s, D1957-60, were delivered in blue livery as were several of the BR Type 2s from D7660. These included the use of a new style font for numbering which was to become the standard for at least the next 20 years. Livery anomalies continued to appear.

The frugal Western Region continued to repaint its shunters in green to use up paint stocks whilst turning out D3460 in blue, as it was a Southern Region allocated loco. Initial blue repaints in the main had yellow panels, but a new standard of full yellow ends applied from mid-year with these also being applied to engines still in green.

With the number of steam engines still operating exceeding 1,000, the last thing that most enthusiasts were expecting was a large cull of modern traction and yet starting in February that is exactly what happened, with the Midland Region withdrawing 29 of the smaller diesel shunters and making the D29XX 300hp class extinct at a stroke.

The Eastern Region included 350hp shunters in its withdrawal list as did the Midland. Whilst most enthusiasts had just viewed the latter as a homogeneous class of 1,193 units there were differences in the power units employed and those not fitted with English Electric engines were targeted in the withdrawal process. The ten Crossley engined examples were

Displaying the new look, D7662/3 pose at Willesden on December 4, 1966. The new style font appeared briefly in combination with the D prefix which was omitted from the end of 1968. Colour-Rail.com

Nearing completion at Crewe in August was the pioneer Class 74 (as they became) in the shape of E6101 - rebuilt from an E5000 to include a 650hp diesel motor. F Hornby/Colour-Rail.com

The latest thing in 1960s coaching stock, this being a First Class compartment model. Colour-Rail.com

1967

eliminated as were those with Blackstone engines in combination with BTH traction equipment. Next in line would be the Blackstone/GEC machines. The Scottish Region joined the party in March with 26 shunters withdrawn, almost all of them being from the North British built D27XX design. The pace of withdrawal of DMU stock also hotted up with the original Derby and Metro Cammell lightweight units being targeted.

However, the sting in the tail came towards the year end with the condemnation of the first of BR's 'less successful' main line types with Metrovicks D5700/3/4/9.10/3 being at the front of the queue, not even being retained to see off steam. Right behind them were D600-4 and D6301 from the Western and no less than 31 D61XX from Scotland. However, much more scandalous was the removal from stock of D9522/31, and the fate of this class would in due course be picked up by the national press.

The stock of railbuses continued to dwindle, but rather than being scrapped a number of these found a new life on fledgling heritage lines. Some DMU sets were being 'repurposed' at this time, with seats being removed and then branded as parcels cars. Some EMUs were also being withdrawn with a thinning of the stock used on the Manchester-Altrincham services.

The reduction in the number of locomotives based on the Western Region continued, with further batches of EE Type 3s going to the Eastern Region and Brush Type 4s going to the Midland.

A recent development at Swindon works was the provision of a set of condemned coaching stock to form a test train for use in trialling locomotives that had been out shopped after overhaul.

A benefit of the Bournemouth electrification was that electric multiple units overhauled at Eastleigh could now get to and from the works under their own power.

The first 4VEP units for stopping services on the Waterloo- ➤

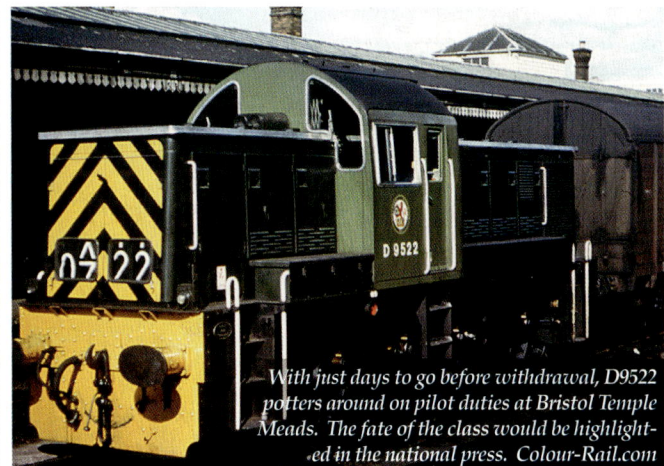

Waiting the call to the scrap yard at Crewe are four of the D29XX series of shunters with D2911 nearest the camera. None completed ten years of service. Colour-Rail.com

With just days to go before withdrawal, D9522 potters around on pilot duties at Bristol Temple Meads. The fate of the class would be highlighted in the national press. Colour-Rail.com

Britain's Railways in the 1960s
61

On the final day of through services from Paddington, 92234 is waiting at Birkenhead Woodside to work one of the specials returning to London as far as Chester with 42616 on pilot duties. Colour-Rail.com

Bournemouth route were noted on delivery in April and soon entered passenger service.

The Newhaven boat train had long been worked by one of the Southern electric locos 20001-3 but in the spring the service acquired a set of blue and grey coaching stock in combination with a blue painted electro diesel.

A new class for North East England was the EE Type 1, with new builds from D8300 arriving in blue livery, these ensuring the removal of Claytons from the area.

The ex-London Transport tube stock for use on the Isle of Wight comprised six three-car sets designated as 3 TIS and numbered 031-036 and six four-car sets as 4 VEC 041-046.

A plan to see Warships taking over duties based in Birmingham saw D836/46 arrive in the area for driver training. In the event, whilst they did take over Paddington services from October 1, they were allocated to Old Oak Common rather than Midland sheds. However, their sojourn on the route did not last long with Brush Type 4s returning before the end of the year.

Other Warships on the move were some of the D600s with D601/2 being transferred to Landore for freight duties. However, their stay in Wales did not last long on this occasion, unlike when two of them ended up at Barry dock for scrap.

The first of the new design of Type 4 locomotive, D400, was delivered in October and was allocated to 'Western Lines' and carried a plate stating that it was the property of English Electric Holdings Ltd.

New locomotives delivered in the year comprised D1108-11, D1957-60, D7667-77, D8185-99, and D8300-18/20-5 along with electro diesel E6049. D400/1/2/4 were considered as 'hired locomotives. Rebuilt were E6102/3 from E5016/06. Diesel withdrawals totalled 286 of which 70 were 350hp shunters and 170 of the smaller varieties.

Steam Happenings

At January 1, 1967, no fewer than 67 sheds still had a steam allocation. BR Standard Class 70013 *Oliver Cromwell* was out-shopped at Crewe on February 2 and was officially the last steam engine to be returned to traffic from the works. Unlike recent repaints, it was fully lined out and gloss painted. However, Crewe was still working on 60010 *Dominion of Canada* and 92220 *Evening Star* for preservation.

Vale of Rheidol services were to be run from the old Platform 1 of

The use of the North British Warships on services from Birmingham to the capital was brief. Even shorter was the period when those services were diverted to Marylebone to facilitate the completion of a re-signalling programme. D850 Swift stands at Marylebone on November 4, 1967. J L Lean/Colour-Rail.com

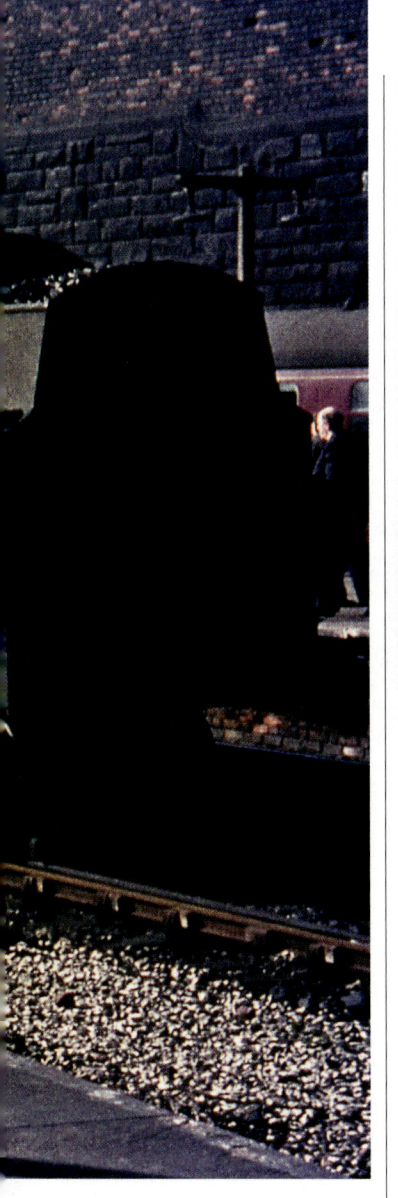

The end of steam in Scotland seemed to attract little public attention. B1 61340 gives some trucks a run out at Dundee on March 25, less than four weeks before it was withdrawn. Colour-Rail.com

the main station with the original terminus station closed, but in the end this change was postponed for a year.

March 1967 saw the withdrawal of through services from Paddington to Birmingham and beyond to Birkenhead. These had been steam-hauled from Shrewsbury onwards. The final day of services was marked by the running of two specials from London, both Castle-powered as far as Chester using the by now preserved 4079 and 7029. The Cambrian Coast Express had also stayed steam worked to this point by 75XXX BR Standards, one of the few named trains on BR to have steam power by this date. Shrewsbury shed closed with the cessation of these services thus also eliminating steam from the Cambrian lines.

Steam engines allocated to Scottish sheds were by now used almost entirely on freight duties with several of the aged J36 and J37 0-6-0s still hard at work, with B1s and WDs making up most of the rest of the fleet.

At the end of 1966 steam trains had finished on the Isle of Wight with passenger services suspended whilst the system was electrified, with most of the fleet of O2 0-4-4 tanks condemned. However, W24 and W31 were retained in traffic to assist in the required permanent way work. This was completed in March when both were withdrawn thus rendering the class extinct.

The former North Eastern Region was likewise experiencing the last rights with a total steam stock of 124 units in early July. Just 35 engines remained active in County Durham and at North Blyth with the rest concentrated around Leeds.

The writing was also clearly on the wall in Scotland with nearly half the remaining steam stock withdrawn in April leaving just 30 locomotives flying the flag north of the border. Clayton diesels took on the former steam pilot duties at Glasgow Central and the Beattock bankers were due to be replaced on May 1. However, much steam power still lurked on the region, with many withdrawn engines still at sheds with Scottish scrap merchants also dealing in locomotives from south of the border. The end for operational steam based in Scotland came just a month later, the last two engines in stock being veterans 65288 and 65345, although these were in store at the time pending possible use on a filming contract. Polmadie remained open to steam however as some trains were still being steam worked from Carlisle and even Perth was available to deal with steam if necessary.

Despite the demise of Southern steam being less than two months away, steam shunting duties continued in Southampton docks with 30067/9 being active in May. The chronicling of the movements of 77014, for long hidden away at Guildford since its transfer to the Southern Region, started to appear in the press with it being noted on a Weymouth-Bournemouth passenger duty on May 18.

If Scottish steam had gone out with barely a whimper, the end of Southern steam was extensively covered in the press. Some 80 engines remained on the books until the last weekend and high speed exploits continued. Special 'last steam' trains were laid on by BR. It seems that the final steam run was performed by 77014 on a parcels train.

The demise of steam traction also spelt the end of the Bournemouth Belle. Electrification did not however mean the end of locomotive-hauled services as both the Channel Islands and Southampton boat trains remained, being worked by anything from an Electro diesel to a Brush Type 4. Whilst the focus had been on the mainline services, steam-worked empty stock duties at Waterloo ceased and the Clapham-Kensington Olympia service became a diesel loco turn. Salisbury was chosen as an assembly point for most of the withdrawn engines before they were gradually removed for scrap.

A 'last stand for steam' again saw summer Saturday trains over the S&C route diagrammed for Jubilee haulage until August 26. 45562 *Alberta* had been employed on a railtour that took it to Hartlepool in May. ➤

The engine that brought down the curtain on Southern steam was BR Standard 77014 which stands forlorn at Bournemouth on the final day, July 9, 1967. G Parry Collection/Colour-Rail.com

Britain's Railways in the 1960s

With the closure of Crewe South shed to steam in November, nearly all steam activity was concentrated in the Lancashire and Cumbria area, with only Northwich and Buxton sheds being outside these counties. To this end the rate of steam withdrawals on the Midland Region ramped up considerably towards the end of the year with few Britannias surviving the October and November cuts and all falling at the end of December except for 70013 *Oliver Cromwell* which moved from Carlisle to Carnforth, where it saw use almost exclusively on railtours.

Steam withdrawals in the year left few classes at work into 1968 with much of the stock comprising Stanier 5MTs and 8Fs.

Infrastructure and Rolling Stock

Another investment in computers and new offices was announced with a scheme to build a 13 storey office block at Crewe and a £0.5m programme of track improvements associated with London Bridge was undertaken from early in the year. The improvements were so that additional trains could run at peak hours from July. This included the provision of new carriage sidings at Blackfriars and a turn back siding as far out as Sidcup. A four year programme to rebuild Ashford station was almost completed by February.

A new diesel depot opened at Knottingley, primarily to serve the MGR services to Ferrybridge and other local power stations, its initial allocation being just six Brush Type 4s. Work began on the final new depots at Cambois near Blyth and at Kingmoor, with the latter well advanced by April. Following an upgrade of facilities at the old ex-GWR shed at Exeter, the Southern Region's Exmouth Junction depot was closed.

A Freightliner terminal was opened on a site two miles east of Cardiff General on June 30 despite the first train running ten days earlier. This was the first such facility in Wales. A terminal in Dudley was opened on October 1 with services to Glasgow, Newcastle, and Southampton. Another terminal under construction was that at Millbrook near Southampton.

Plans were also announced in August to close St Pancras station with suburban services running to Moorgate and mainline trains to Euston.

Services

Freightliner trains were to be introduced on the Western region as were additional car carrying trains. The long-established Condor freight service between Hendon and Glasgow ceased in November and was replaced by freight liners on the West Coast route.

Railair services were enhanced and changed. The link at Slough for trains to the west was to be moved to Reading where up to 80 trains would call each day. The Slough service had carried 17,000 passengers in its first year.

Full electric services to Birmingham and Wolverhampton commenced from March running hourly with a time of 94 minutes to Birmingham compared to the previous journey time of two hours. Alternate trains ran forward to Manchester and Liverpool. A small number of AM10 units were still to be delivered at the start of the year, but all were available for the March date to allow full electrification of the various secondary and local services. Such was the success of the new services from Coventry that additional trains were already having to be run with patronage up 100% in the first six weeks.

With completion of the West Coast scheme, Birmingham-London services would also operate out of New Street to Paddington six times daily calling at High Wycombe to use the already established Heathrow link from there.

Service withdrawals took place on January 2 on the Tunbridge Wells-Three Bridges, Cambridge-Sudbury and Kilmarnock-Barrasie lines. Local services finished between Ipswich and Norwich and Leeds Central was closed. Bodmin-Wadebridge-Padstow closed at the end of January whilst Sidmouth lost its trains in March as did Appledore to New Romney. The Great Central closure of 1966 had left a skeleton

Railtour duty for Jubilee 45562 **Alberta** *took it to unusual territory on May 6 when it was serviced at Hartlepool shed. G Parry Collection/Colour-Rail.com*

Early in 1967 a scheme was announced to increase capacity for services using London Bridge station. Seen before work commenced, 4 COR 3112 approaches the station. Colour-Rail.com

64   *Britain's Railways in the 1960s*

service operating from Rugby to Nottingham, but this was clearly being lined up for closure in 1967 and indeed Nottingham Victoria closed in September with services then temporarily terminating at Arkwright Street. Birkenhead Woodside station closed on November 4, 1967 with Rock Ferry becoming the interchange point between services from Chester and the Merseyside electrics. Other notable casualties were the local services between Derby/Nottingham and Sheffield and York-Pontefract. Several other lines closed but were at the time 'freight only.'

The Clayfreighter service proposed in 1966 started to operate to Sittingbourne from Cornwall on February 24.

In late summer, the Liverpool division reported a 50% increase in trade on its car carrying services and that it was running more than 500 company freight trains per week.

The year saw the introduction of a number of additional routes where guards issued tickets on the train following the closure of station booking offices and in due course these became wide spread and christened 'Pay Trains.'

In a textbook example of 'how to kill a station' BR applied to close Brent Knoll, between Weston-super-Mare and Highbridge. This had been specifically rejected by the Minister of Transport back in 1964 when it was served by six trains daily, but now had but one.

New trains to try and boost the Motorail market were introduced between Cardiff and St Austell. The timing of this may not have been best with the new Severn Bridge having just opened, thus reducing driving time considerably.

The famed 60 minute timing of nonstop trains between London and Brighton, which dated back to Southern Railway days, was finally breached in the summer timetable with several trains being scheduled to complete the run in 55 minutes.

Throughout the country cuts in Sunday services were notable which, when combined with the frequent weekend engineering works, made many journeys undesirable.

New electrified routes came into operation from Glasgow being the services to Gourock and Wemyss Bay. Journey times were substantially reduced, and train mileage increased by around 50%. Some trains entered service from June 5, but the full timetable did not start until September.

Due to re-signalling at Paddington the newly introduced services from Birmingham were diverted to Marylebone in October and November. This also led to the appearance there of NBL Type 2s on ECS duties.

A programme to fit many vacuum brake-only locomotives with air brakes was started.

One effect of the rationalisation of the Salisbury-Exeter route and the closure of the Taunton-Barnstaple line was that through trains to Ilfracombe had to run via the Great Western route to Exeter and reverse at Exeter St Davids.

The electrified service on the Isle of Wight ran at anything from 12-60 minute frequency depending on the time and season with all sets being required in traffic on the summer Saturdays.

Observations

At the start of 1967, on the Waterloo-Bournemouth route, six trains were rostered for a Brush Type 4, four to be worked by a D65XX with the new 4 TC stock and eight for steam. Work on the electrification saw the remodelling of track at Bournemouth station with both platform lines signalled for reversible working with the through lines removed. From April some trains became fully electric worked, powered by the ▶

AM10 unit 061 runs into the fully rebuilt Euston in September. Colour-Rail.com

D1670 Mammoth heads the Clayfreighter, conveying liquid china clay from Cornwall to Kent past Keyham in April. Colour-Rail.com

Unusually entrusted with passenger duties was Ivatt 4MT 43033 seen at Preston on July 28, 1967. M H Yardley/Colour-Rail.com

new 4 REP units which were used in combination with one or two of the unpowered 4 TC sets. This reduced the number of booked steam express duties to just two on Mondays to Fridays. The route had also seen the passage of the final Pines Express on March 4. The prospect of the end of steam seemed to spur some locomotive crews to see just what performance could be extracted from a run down Bulleid Pacific and a number of runs saw trains exceed 90mph with a small number achieving an authenticated, but definitely against the rules, 100 mph.

Observations at Dawlish in June found that Monday-Friday services were almost all worked by Warships or Westerns but on Saturdays several Peaks and Brush Type 4s appeared. Hymeks were noticeable by their absence.

BR continued to offer tickets for impossible journeys. Noted at Bromsgrove was an advert for a day return to Worcester. Unfortunately, the only train to Worcester ran at 17.59 with the return trip not possible until the next day. The biennial Scotland v Wales Rugby match at Murrayfield brought nine excursions to Edinburgh, four of which were in the hands of Western Region Brush Type 4s, all nine arriving via the Waverley route.

As the year progressed, Preston became established as the place to see steam on passenger duties, particularly on specials and extras, with for instance the Thursday before Easter producing eight such trains worked by Stanier Class 5s and Britannias.

However, on the same weekend Huddersfield was another place where steam was still active and on the same Thursday it saw six steam-hauled passenger services, all with Class 5 power and the next day a visitor to Wakefield shed found 61 steam engines present of which no fewer than 29 were WD 2-8-0s.

The summer timetable saw up to 30 steam-hauled passenger trains on Saturdays at Preston, almost exclusively in the hands of Stanier Class 5s. Another location where there were regular steam passenger duties, but on a vastly different scale, was at Bradford where the portions of trains to Kings Cross, that joined the main service at Huddersfield, enjoyed the services of ex LMS 2-6-4 tanks, even on Pullman trains.

On September 9, 1967, the last steam engines were withdrawn from County Durham and other

Type 2 7504 double heads a train from Ilfracombe into Exeter St Davids whilst a Western waits to come on at the other end to take the train to Paddington. This arrangement had become necessary following the closure of the direct route to Taunton. Colour-Rail.com

66   Britain's Railways in the 1960s

On the penultimate day of North East steam Q6 63387 gives of its best one more time as it works coal empties near Hart Junction. Colour-Rail.com

withdrawals reduced the Eastern steam stock to just 21 engines, primarily being 17 Stanier 8Fs at Royston. Q6s 63387/95 and J27s 65811/24/94 were the last engines in action of their respective classes.

The remaining steam allocation in West Yorkshire was almost eliminated on November 4 with 48222 carrying out the final duty, thus leaving all active steam locomotives allocated to the Midland Region. A strange solo survivor was K1 62005 which was in store and was officially withdrawn on December 30. However, at that time it had found gainful temporary employment, as it was supplying steam at the ICI North Tees site, due to an equipment failure there, a task that it undertook for six weeks, being in due course rescued for preservation.

A visit to York shed in November found no fewer than 34 204hp shunters gathered, some of which were designated for conversion in the pairing up programme.

On March 25 what was perhaps the longest passenger train since World War Two had run on the Scottish Region. Loaded to 18 coaches this was double-headed from Edinburgh to Perth by D368 and D1973 where they handed over to 44997 and the by now privately owned 60009 to work far as Aberdeen.

A diesel leg took the train to Keith and Aviemore and back to Perth where the steam combination returned the train to Edinburgh. The total mileage exceeded 500, all for a fare of £2.50. Even better value was a summer Mystery Excursion from Weston-super-Mare to Clacton with 440 miles of travel enjoyed for a fare of just £1.

From April 3 the last steam operated branch line, that to Lymington, was turned over to electric power with 80152 being the final steam engine to work the service.

On May 13 Crewe South shed contained more than 70 steam engines but 30 of them were in store, likewise at Stoke where 50% of the 36 residents were not in traffic. On September 9, Kingmoor shed was host to over 80 steam engines but only nine were actually in steam. The shed was expected to close on December 31.

The Pullman stock introduced on the Midland Region was painted in reverse of the normal coaching livery i.e. grey with blue window surrounds from new. The diesel Pullman sets also acquired this livery on repaint in 1967.

What became some of the most difficult diesels on the system to be underlined in the spotting books were D2954/5, which were moved to the isolated system on Holyhead breakwater, where they replaced a longstanding departmental engine, ED6. A trip around Scottish sheds in early September found a dismal picture for the NBL Type 2s with 17 of the final 20 in store, many in locked and bricked up sheds. Several of the earlier batch were also seen resting peacefully at various locations.

A breed of coaching stock that was disappearing rapidly was the suburban coach, i.e. ones with no corridor connections and in most cases composed entirely of compartments, despite many of them having been built only in the early 1950s.

It was said that many of the under-frames had been used to form the expanding fleet of car flats. There had also been a major purge of carriages built just prior to the introduction of the BR Standard design although the number in traffic was still well into four figures.

The open days held at Bristol Bath Road shed continued and on October 21 the attendance was said to be more than 10,000 people. As well as the modern traction on show, a few steam engines appeared. Some such as 46201 *Princess Elizabeth* by invite but West Countries 34013 and 34100 were borrowed from a passing scrap train.

And there was a tragic incident late in 1967 when the 19.43 DEMU from Hastings to London on November 5 left the track due to a broken rail. The crash occurred between Grove Park and Hither Green whilst the train was travelling at around 70mph and resulted in 49 deaths and 78 injuries. ∎

Rostered to work one of the longest trains of the decade, an 18 coach, 500 mile railtour, were Stanier 5MT and the now privately owned A4 60009. Here they wait for action at Perth. T Owen/Colour-Rail.com

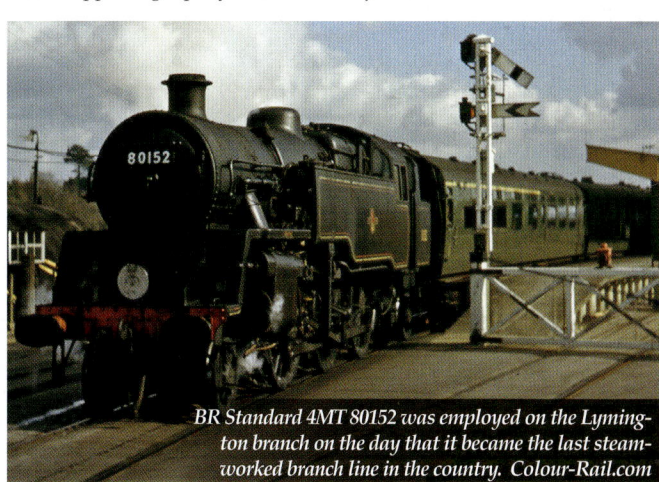

BR Standard 4MT 80152 was employed on the Lymington branch on the day that it became the last steam-worked branch line in the country. Colour-Rail.com

Britain's Railways in the 1960s

1968
OVERVIEW

The big event at the start of the year was Dr Richard Beeching leaving the railways to return to ICI. He left a legacy that is still talked about today. His replacement, H C Johnson was appointed as the new chairman from January 1.

The year opened with almost 5,100 diesel and electric locomotives on the books but just a mere 362 steam engines, the end for these clearly being in sight. Diesel and electric unit carriages exceeded 11,400.

A new classification system was introduced in mid-year which allocated a number to each class of locomotive from 1-55 for diesels and 70-86 for electric/electro diesels. Generally increasing horse power came with increasing class number. Some numbers were not used. These of course went on to become the basis of the TOPS system, although the revised numbering of locomotives did not start until the early 1970s. Appearing at the same time was a data panel that would be applied to each engine giving basic details such as weight, brake force and route availability.

On Western Region based engines this replaced the route availability coloured disc that had adorned cabsides from way back in the steam era. Hot on the heels of the classification information came the announcement that, as steam traction was now eliminated, diesel locomotives would no longer carry a 'D' prefix to their numbers although electrics would still be denoted by 'E'.

Project successes were not often recorded for public consumption, but the West Coast electrification was an exception, where in 12 months passenger numbers had risen by 45% overall with Coventry to Liverpool and Manchester journeys up by 90%

A dispute leading to a nationwide work to rule took place in June causing widespread disruption and cancellation of services, particularly at weekends due to a ban on overtime and rest day working.

A relatively small electrification scheme in East Anglia was that of the Cheshunt line where work proceeded for most of the year. At the year end the removal of steam power had indeed been completed whilst the rationalisation of the network was still work in progress, with some of the larger issues still to be resolved. Indeed, vast swathes of the system were still loss making.

Modern Traction Scene
Traditionally, other than shunters out stabled at goods yards, locomotives were kept at sheds, either specially built or at former steam sheds. However, with the former often being quite small and the latter being abandoned, the use of holding sidings, often some distance from a depot, started to increase. For instance, at Bescot most out of use locos were stabled on lines some quarter of a mile from the shed.

The 4 REP units used on Waterloo-Bournemouth services gave more problems than the average for Southern EMUs and seemed particularly prone to losing their shoe gear. Units had been seen at Chart Leacon, believed to be receiving modifications to overcome the problem. The buffet cars on these units carried names but they only appeared on the

One of the data panels that appeared on all locomotives but in this case, it is shown after the renumbering of 4501 in the TOPS scheme that was introduced in the 1970s. Colour-Rail.com

1968

27002 was soon to end its BR career but the class would find further employment in The Netherlands. It is seen here at Manchester Piccadilly waiting to go to Sheffield Victoria. T Owen/Colour-Rail.com

4 REP 3003 is ready to depart from Bournemouth to London. They initially had problems with pick up shoes becoming dislodged and were sent to Ashford Works for modification. G Pratt/Colour-Rail.com

mirror behind the counter in each buffet car.

The new EMUs were not the only electrics in trouble with E3036-45 in store at Bury due to problems with their rectifiers whilst several of the Woodhead locos were stored as surplus to requirements. Despite Waterloo effectively now being an all-electric station, the third rail did not extend to the buffer stops at some of the platforms. This posed problems if an electro diesel was in use and at the rear of a departing train, in that it would not have third rail contact. Whilst it could use its diesel engine to move the train, it could not supply current for the heating and lighting, causing passengers to have to board trains that were in darkness in winter months.

Crew training commenced on the new D400s with D402 being based at Polmadie. A modification noted already was that jumper cables had been removed from locomotive ends.

The 1966/7 experiments with double headed EE Types 3s on Western Region expresses was short lived. Now plans emerged for Warships to work in pairs which saw the refitting of multiple working connectors that had been removed over time. Only Swindon-built examples were to be rostered and were working on some duties from early April with usually two pairs employed each day.

The attack on the stock of modern traction motive power which started in 1967 continued. The Eastern Region removed one of the newest of the 350hp shunters, D4080, from traffic as well as the first of the North British Type 1s to go, D8404 along with many Drewry-built 204hp shunters. In March, the region withdrew all of their D95XX locos removing well over half the class in one go. The by-now few remaining examples of the class were working almost exclusively in South Wales. The first condemnation of a Swindon-built Warship was that of D801 which had already run more than 1,000,000 miles. The D57XX Metrovicks were rendered extinct in September swiftly followed by what had only just been designated as class 77, E27001-6.

Next to head for the scrap yard were more than 20 of the D85XX Claytons. Further classes targeted were the Baby Deltics and the D82XX Type 1s (Class 15), the latter being replaced by D80XX transferred from Scotland. With the condemnation of several D63XX, the Western Region needed some replacements, the first of which, D5535 arrived in November.

A start was made on withdrawing some older Southern EMUs such as the 4LAV sets.

The first recorded duties of the D400s saw them employed on the Midday Scot on occasions from Crewe northwards and by the end of 1968 they were working most of the regular services. The E61XX electro diesels, some of which had been out for six months, commenced revenue earning duties on May 6 but initially suffered from very poor availability.

The Midland Region again revised its depot coding system deleting D14 and D15 (replaced by D01) along with ML and WL and added D08 for Liverpool, D09 for Manchester, and D10 for Preston.

Several of the 52XXX series of Swindon-built cross country units were transferred to the London area and put to work on the secondary long distance services from Paddington to Thames Valley destinations replacing Hymek duties.

An economy measure introduced in October 1968 was to work North Wales' coast expresses with pairs of Type 2s rather than a Type 4 diesel. However, the failure rate of the smaller locos was so high that the scheme was abandoned after just four weeks.

At the end of the year the modern traction locomotive stock had seen a reduction in ➤

The new Type 4 locomotives worked many of the expresses north of Crewe and worked through to Windermere which at that time retained its Euston services. Here we see D430 on arrival. G Parry Collection/Colour-Rail.com

Britain's Railways in the 1960s

With relatively minor damage, in better times D6345 would be repaired and returned to service but in 1968 the next stop would be the scrap yard. It is seen here at Old Oak Common. Colour-Rail.com

numbers that exceeded that of the steam fleet. Just 50 new locomotives had been delivered, these being D403/5-49, D1961 and D8319/22/7, with the only other arrivals being 29 EMUs for the Southern Region. No fewer than 422 diesel locomotives were withdrawn. Made extinct were the prototype Swindon Warships, the Metrovicks, unrebuilt NBL diesel Electric Type 2s and the D84XX series. Major inroads were made into the Claytons with 46 being withdrawn as well as 22 D63XX and 43 D95XX.

No fewer than 98 of the 350hp shunters had also been condemned along with 141 of the smaller variety. Two of the E3000 electrics came to grief in accidents and joined 20001-3 and 27001-6 as electric loco withdrawals. Also taken out of service were 161 DMU cars.

Steam Happenings

Carlisle area sheds had closed at the year end with only the following remaining open by January 1. The number of locomotives allocated to each are shown in brackets. Remaining open were 6F Aberystwyth (3-narrow gauge), 8A Edge Hill (37), 8C Speke Junction (25), 8E Northwich (17), 9B Stockport (22), 9D Newton Heath (37), 9E Trafford Park (21), 9F Heaton Mersey (26), 9H Patricroft (36), 9K Bolton (19), 9L Buxton (7), 10A Carnforth (32), 10D Lostock Hall (23), and 10F Rose Grove (27).

In addition, 30 engines that had been allocated to the Carlisle area sheds remained on the official stock list. The above comprised 151 Stanier 5MTs and 150 8Fs with the other types remaining being Standard 7MT, 5MT 4MT and 9F, plus six Ivatt 4MTs and the three Vale of Rheidol engines.

Despite almost all engines now being allocated west of the Pennines, steam still ran through to West Yorkshire, and even on occasions to Sheffield in the early part of the year.

Buxton shed closed on March 2 and Edge Hill, Speke Junction, Stockport, and Heaton Mersey, all closed on May 6 plus the remaining Manchester area depots on July 1 leaving just Carnforth, Rose Grove and Lostock Hall operational.

As of March 7, 1968, there were nine scheduled Class 1 passenger duties for steam, all appearing at Preston except for the 03.32 Leeds-Halifax and the 04.38 Halifax-Manchester trains.

The application of BR blue to some of the steam fleet was newsworthy, although this only applied to the three Vale of Rheidol locomotives. However, a begrimed

The diesels invade as the last day of steam approaches at Lostock Hall shed. Colour-Rail.com

1968

The last steam hauled Belfast Boat Express ran on May 5, 1968 and is seen at Manchester Victoria with 5MT 45025 in charge. Colour-Rail.com

Stanier 5MT was noted in service at Manchester with the double arrow logo chalked on its tender.

The end of steam working had been announced for August and from April onwards various farewell railtours were organised. Understandably, 70013 was used with some regularity whilst most others use Stanier 5MTs although Standard 73069 was also turned out. Double heading was a feature of many such trips. The last named train to use steam power was the Belfast Boat Express, with 45025 used on the official last day of steam on the service, May 5. The area around Preston remained the focus for steam duties.

The last month of steam workings were less than hoped for due, in part, to both a work to rule and the fact that the main holiday weeks had started in the area, reducing freight traffic. Isolated passenger workings still occurred but many duties were on transfer freights. All the remaining BR Standard engines were allocated to Carnforth with the 75XXX working until the end.

The 'last rites' for steam took place on August 4, 1968, one week ahead of the BR sponsored 15 Guinea special.

At Rose Grove the last two engines to come on shed were 48519 and 48773. What is thought to have been the last steam-hauled freight saw 75019 taking a train of vans from Heysham at 16.00 on August 3.

On passenger duties, 45318 took the last timetabled duty on the same day with the 21.25 Preston-Liverpool. Several railtours were run on August 4 with 44871/94 and 44874 plus 45017 on another, both noted at Sefton Junction. 70013 was also active along with 44781, 45025, 45156, 45390, 48476 and 73069, with engines being shared between some trains.

The BR tour on August 11 utilised 45110 on the first and final legs with 44781 plus 44871 and 70013 completing the line-up. Vast crowds lined the route with roads on the Settle & Carlisle portion blocked by parked cars.

Steam engine condemnations at 359 eliminated the main line fleet and almost all withdrawn engines had been removed to scrap yards by the end of the year except for 15 at Lostock Hall. The British Railways steam fleet thus stood at just the three Vale of Rheidol locomotives.

Infrastructure and Rolling Stock

Many stabling and signing on points in South Wales were targeted for closure during the year. Proposals were put forward to single much of the route from Wolverhampton-Shrewsbury and on to Chester with most remaining stations being reduced to unstaffed status.

The Royal Albert Bridge connecting Cornwall and Devon had to be upgraded to take the weight of the Freightliner trains running from Par and the Severn rail bridge which had been closed in 1960 after being hit by a barge was demolished during 1967/8. All the steel structure had been removed by the end of 1968 and seven of the 13 pillars were blown up on March 10, 1969.

The Cambrian route from Welshpool became single line with passing loops following the removal of one track between Newtown and Welshpool. The new terminal arrangements for the Vale of Rheidol line were used for the first time at Whitsun. The Vale of Rheidol engines then used the former standard gauge shed which was also used for carriage repair work. A record 48,540 passengers were carried on the line during the season.

Re-signalling was planned for the Bristol area with a new signal box to be built in the old station area. Completion was scheduled for 1971. Re-signalling at Swindon saw the closure of the downside platforms.

A new station was opened at ➤

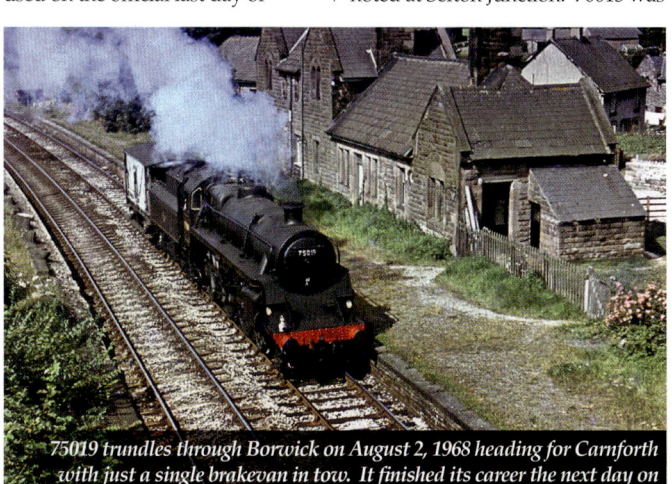

75019 trundles through Borwick on August 2, 1968 heading for Carnforth with just a single brakevan in tow. It finished its career the next day on what is thought to be the last steam hauled freight on BR. Colour-Rail.com

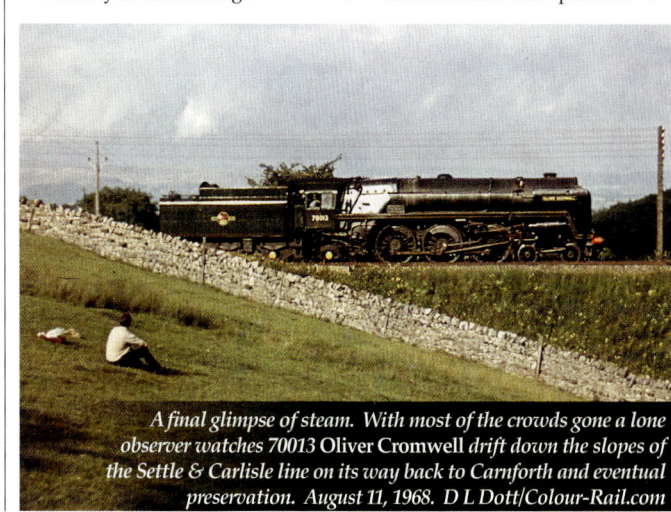

A final glimpse of steam. With most of the crowds gone a lone observer watches 70013 Oliver Cromwell drift down the slopes of the Settle & Carlisle line on its way back to Carnforth and eventual preservation. August 11, 1968. D L Dott/Colour-Rail.com

Crawley, being a replacement for the existing one but being very slightly nearer to London.

Services

The year started with a number of major closure proposals still in the air such as Exeter-Ilfracombe, the remains of the Great Central line, the Central Wales line, Birmingham-Wolverhampton and many associated services that used Snow Hill, Manchester Central and Exchange. A significant line closure took effect from January 1, this being the route from Oxford to Cambridge with just Bletchley to Bedford remaining open.

A new proposal was to close Fenchurch Street on weekdays, after the evening peak and run trains into Liverpool Street instead. And March 21 saw the curtain come down on passenger services between Stratford on Avon and Cheltenham.

The former Southern route from Exeter to Plymouth via Okehampton closed on May 5, 1968. Penarth to Cadoxton was another casualty at this time. From August 22 Birmingham Snow Hill station was only open from 06.00-09.00 and 15.45 until 18.00. The southern approach to the station was severed in November when sections of track in the tunnel were removed. Despite the closure of the North Warwickshire route from Stratford to Birmingham via Henley in Arden being approved by the minister of transport, local opposition forced another enquiry to be launched which started on September 11.

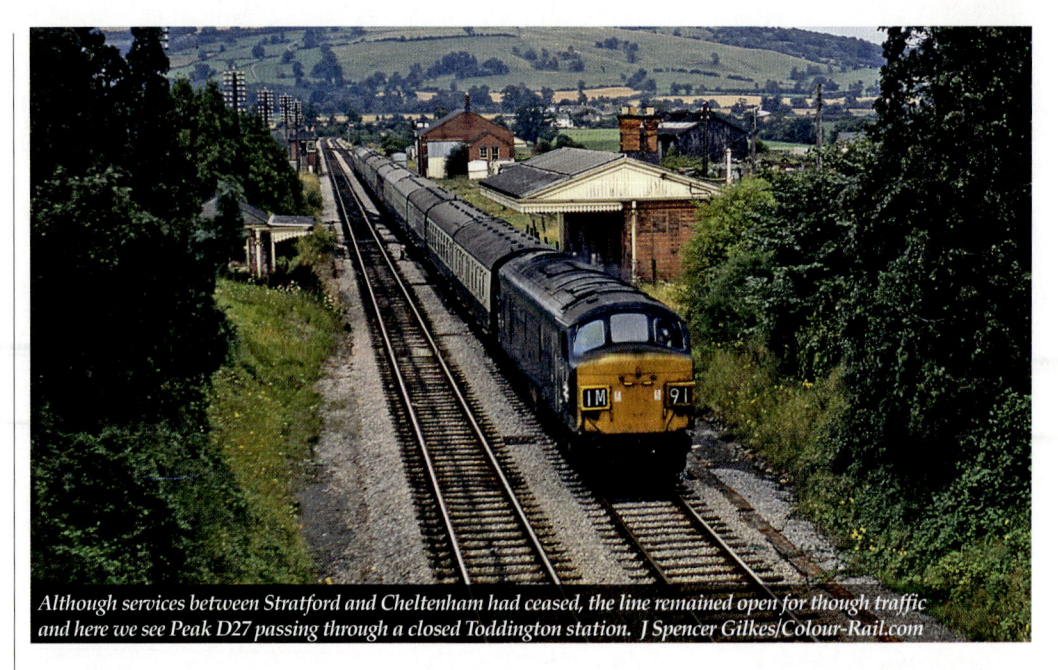

Once again, 'disincentives' to travel were employed to help the case for closure, this time on the Ilfracombe line where connections at Exeter with services to/from London, via either route, generally involved a wait of more than 30 minutes.

Plans were announced for a further acceleration of services to the West Country with the start of the summer timetable with the Cornish Riviera Express reaching Plymouth in 3hrs 45 minutes with two stops.

Millbrook Freightliner terminal commenced commercial operation on January 29 starting with a train to Stratford, soon followed by a service to Dudley. Despite all the positive news about Freightliner trains, general freight traffic was in sharp decline. A survey at Huddersfield noted 29 freights on October 22 compared with 120 two years earlier.

An interesting new freight contract was for the carrying of 500,000 tons of steel just 13 miles between Brierley Hill and Wednesfield over a five year period. The canal had also been considered but rail won the contract as sending via the waterways involved double handling. Also, a £650,000 deal to run to the end of 1969 was signed with the Rootes group to move car bodies between Coventry and Linwood.

Passenger services from Coventry to London were increased again from May 6 but Rugby, once a key station on the line, gradually saw a reduction in trains that called.

The summer timetable showed that the fastest train in Britain was on the West Coast route where the 07.45 from Euston-Liverpool ran non-stop from Watford to Runcorn at an average speed of 82.3 mph.

The five per day through train service from Portsmouth to Cardiff was reduced to just two per day from May 6.

Observations

Another major accident occurred on January 6, 1968 when a West Coast electric ploughed into a lorry carrying a 110 ton transformer which was on a level crossing at Hixon. Eleven people were killed.

Both Gloucester and Shrewsbury temporarily became staging posts for steam engines making their way to South Wales for scrapping. Some locomotives rested for periods exceeding two weeks. Despite Southern steam having finished in July 1967, sales of locomotives from Salisbury were still being made well into the first half of 1968

Regular cross regional boundary diesel workings, particularly on freight, continued to grow. An example was the use of a Cardiff based Brush Type 4 on a Severn Tunnel Junction to Temple Mills

Although services between Stratford and Cheltenham had ceased, the line remained open for though traffic and here we see Peak D27 passing through a closed Toddington station. J Spencer Gilkes/Colour-Rail.com

The Severn rail bridge was damaged in 1960 and was finally demolished in 1968/9. It is seen herein 1964 with the swing section spanning the Gloucester and Sharpness canal open. T Owen/Colour-Rail

E3009 was the locomotive involved in the Hixon rail crash. Its remains rested at Crewe Works for a while pending a decision on its future. This picture was taken there in May 1968. J B Hall/Colour-Rail.com

While the likes of Coventry saw an improved service following electrification, the once important stopping place, Rugby saw a decline in the number of services that called there. E3145 was seen on a Scotch express in 1966. Colour-Rail.com

freight. However, it was then employed on a passenger turn from Liverpool Street to Norwich before returning home on a Norwich-Bristol freight. With the introduction of a Southampton-Newcastle Freightliner, the latter had diagrammed workings for locomotives from all regions as the Southampton turn brought Eastleigh allocated Type 4s on alternate days. One of two duties for a Western based engine was the 08.15 from Cardiff and return which, whilst booked for a Bath Road Brush, could see examples from any Western depot being used, with repeat performers rarely being noted in four months of observation.

Some diesel diagrams were very complex with for instance an Eastleigh Brush Type 4 being on a five day cycle that would see it appear at Stratford, Newcastle, Kings Cross and Hull working everything from The Hull Pullman to a Class 7 freight before returning to the south coast.

A Western Region punctuality survey claimed that 91% of all Paddington-Bristol services in the week ending February 24 were right time and a London division spot check of 118 trains on March 7 showed that 53 were early and only nine more than five minutes late.

The introduction of air braked stock on the East Coast mainline, and the modification of the Deltics to work with it, saw a major temporary recasting of diagrams to make sure that an air braked example was always on the right diagram to match the stock. Thus, the long standing allocations were juggled such that all the air-braked members of the class were allocated to Finsbury Park. It was hoped that all class members would be air-braked in time for the start of the summer timetable.

Demand on some East Coast services during the summer required the running of trains comprised of up to 14 carriages. As some of the additional carriages were not passed for 100mph running, the combination of heavy trains and the speed restriction caused some late running.

A visit to Woodham's scrap yard at Barry recorded 201 engines present on March 28 and this had risen to 219 by the middle of December.

Not included in the list was 4F 43924 which had departed to the Keighley & Worth Valley railway, being the first engine to be rescued from Woodham's for preservation.

Grand Scottish Tour No. 5 on June 1 proved to be almost anything but, the only part relevant

Occasionally a photographer stood back and recorded the whole scene that was Barry scrap yard in the late 1960s. T Owen/Colour-Rail.com

to Scotland was that it ran to and from Edinburgh. D1773 of Finsbury Park took the train to Carnforth where 70013 worked to Guide Bridge thence 26052 went through to Sheffield Victoria and back. 70013 then headed it to Blackburn and D1773 onwards as far as Stirling. Finally, York based D257 ran back to Edinburgh.

Very heavy rain in the West Country hit services on July 10. At one point Bristol was completely cut off by rail and passengers on the 22.45 Paddington-Bristol ended up arriving in Bristol 15 hours late having spent a night in a transport cafe and finishing their journey by coach. Due to landslides at Flax Bourton, the only service between Taunton and Bristol was a DMU shuttle with all long distance holiday expresses routed via Bath and Westbury to reach Taunton, an unprecedented situation. Diversions remained in place on the following weekend with services running up to two hours late. On September 14/15 large areas of the Southern region were hit by more major flood damage with recovery taking up to a week.

Two excursions from Reading to Margate were DMU worked taking 52XXX cross country units to the Kent coast for the first time. ■

Britain's Railways in the 1960s

1969 OVERVIEW

The government announced that it would support loss making services to the tune of £62m for the year with 135 routes being covered. A further 56 lines were still under review for aid. Whilst the inclusion of a line such as Birmingham-Redditch might have been anticipated, the likes of Liverpool-Warrington-Manchester or Edinburgh-Perth might not have been expected to require a grant.

The year opened with a locomotive fleet numbering 4,375 diesel units, 329 electric and three steam locomotives.

An order for 600 new carriages was placed to a revised design designated as Mk2b. Development work on an experimental gas turbine train was also underway at Derby and was expected to be ready for trials in 1972.

A £30m scheme to rationalise and improve the West Coast route from Weaver Junction to Glasgow was announced. There would be just 24 miles of quadruple track and five signal boxes, with completion scheduled for 1973.

In October, Passenger Transport Authorities were introduced covering the West Midlands, Greater Manchester, Merseyside, West Yorkshire, and Tyneside.

Modern Traction Scene

Delivery of a new batch of 4 VEP units commenced in January and a prototype design of suburban train was also expected on the Southern Region in 1970.

As well as additional Class 31s transferred to the Western Region, February saw the arrival of the first of many Class 46s with Bristol Bath Road receiving the initial allocation. Peaks, but of the class 45 variety, were not a new thing at the shed as D33-42 had been allocated there earlier in the decade.

Another move saw all the Class 27s on the Midland Region move to Scotland.

Some 26XXX locomotives were being fitted for multiple operation with 26007/8/10/24/5/30 noted so fitted in March. The nameplates fitted to Class 40s had started to be removed but possibly by those 'unofficially' carrying a screwdriver rather than by BR staff.

The sorry tale of the D95XX locomotives came to an end in May, just four years after it started, with the final engines being withdrawn. The only positive that could be drawn from this was that many went on to give good service to industry and then have a third life on heritage lines, thus outliving the majority of 1960s motive power.

DMU reallocations saw Swindon-built cross country units moved to Derby and their use on services to Lincoln. In turn this led to a change from DMUs to loco-hauled trains on several routes on the Western Region.

Prior to their designation as Class 48s, 1702-6, which had been fitted with experimental engines were all at Crewe at the end of the year for conversion to conventional Class 47s.

In summary, the motive power fleet changes for the year saw no new locomotives delivered, undoubtedly a first since the advent of steam power. Following the drastic pruning of the previous year, just 174 diesel and electric engines were withdrawn, but a number were re-instated to traffic making the actual change minus 165. Of those most were shunters but the first examples from classes 24 and 43 were notable. Other interesting withdrawals were D830 - the Warship fitted with a 2,400hp Paxman engine, D1908 - an accident victim, E3055 and 26000, the latter being the prototype engine for the Woodhead route.

DMU car withdrawals totalled 157 with no new deliveries, whilst for EMUs 4 VEPs 7756- 7804 arrived and a substantial number of older Southern units from the 2 BIL, 2 HAL and 4 LAV classes were condemned.

Steam Happenings

The only BR steam service remaining was on the Vale of Rheidol line, which carried 52,090 passengers during the 1969 season with the last train worked by No. 9. In response to rumours that a syndicate was trying to buy the line the BR reply simply stated 'there is no intention to sell the line for the foreseeable future.'

However, other steam power did appear during the year. Firstly, there were still steam-powered cranes in use. Frequently unrecorded in earlier years were the occasional appearances of industrial locos on BR metals and these did occur in the year. With the end of mainline steam in 1968, BR imposed a ban on the use of any preserved engine on the system, which however did not apply to 4472 *Flying Scotsman* as Alan Pegler had a contract for its continued use and it worked a number of railtours in the year, but it was shipped to the USA in the autumn,

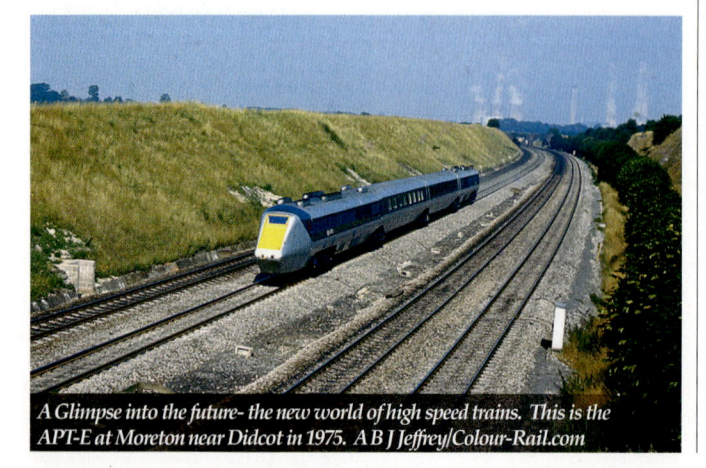

An early casualty of the rationalisation of the diesel fleet was D830 Majestic which looked anything but that on the scrap road at Swindon. It had a non-standard Paxman engine. Colour-Rail.com

A large batch of 4 VEP units were delivered to the Southern Region of which 7783 was one, seen at Brighton in June. Colour-Rail.com

A Glimpse into the future- the new world of high speed trains. This is the APT-E at Moreton near Didcot in 1975. A B J Jeffrey/Colour-Rail.com

Vale of Rheidol 9 Prince of Wales brought down the curtain on operations for the season. It is seen in the 'new' station at Aberystwyth which used to be the bay used for services to Carmarthen. The 'great British summer' weather is evident. Colour-Rail.com

finally removing the steam-hauled passenger train from British Railways.

Infrastructure
A new station was to be built to serve Teesside Airport on the Darlington-Saltburn line. Plans for a new station in Bradford, replacing Exchange were announced, the terminal building also being part of a new bus station with completion due in 1971.

The Southern Region planned to spend £14m on infrastructure work during the year, up from £11m in the previous one. In 1961 it had 33 miles of continuously welded rail, which by 1968 had grown to 530 miles. Colour light signalling was planned for 100 more route miles by the end of 1971 and another new signalling scheme going live was around Nottingham and Derby.

Also, the Lea Valley electrification scheme went live on May 5.

Fifty new carriages for postal services were delivered with some fitted out to both drop and deliver mail but the majority were just fitted with pick-up nets. A further smaller batch were stowage and storing vehicles.

Giving an indication of things to come was the closure on April 5 of Millerhill Up Yard, this being part of a wide-reaching modernisation plan put forward in the 1950s. It was in use for less than ten years.

A new Freightliner depot at Trafford Park was under construction in 1969. Whilst some Freightliner services were struggling for custom, the traffic from Garston required a doubling of capacity and the installation of two large electric overhead cranes.

A project to rebuild Cannon Street station had started in around 1960 but was suspended when only partially complete. Due to a dispute with the local corporation over a road widening scheme it took until 1969 to restart the project.

Much of Birmingham Snow Hill station was demolished in November and December despite still being open for services.

Services
The Waverley route closed on January 4. Unusually the final train met physical opposition with crowds of protestors standing on the line at level crossings whilst threats of other obstructions caused the line to be checked before the final train passed which delayed its arrival in Carlisle by two hours. The Darlington-Richmond route closed March 3.

Permission was granted for the closure of the Swanage branch, but the date was not announced, and it was still open at the end of the year.

The final nail in the Great Central coffin saw services from Rugby-Nottingham withdrawn on May 5.

Service withdrawal proposals continued to surface but there was an increasing trend for the minister of transport to reject them, such as the Central Wales line (again) and Norwich to Sheringham although Wymondham to Dereham was approved.

It was announced that the frequency of Birmingham-London expresses was to be increased to half hourly during the year.

Sleeper services were withdrawn from St Pancras on January 4 and replaced by new services from Euston. Cardiff-Birmingham services via Abergavenny were withdrawn on January 6, notices advising of the change appearing just 24 hours before implementation. The long running wrangle over the closure of the North Warwickshire line rumbled on with closure scheduled for May 5 despite appeals being outstanding. The protest groups obtained an injunction to prevent this pending conclusion of the appeals process and in the next decade achieved their objective.

Manchester Exchange and Central were closed on May 5.

A new line under scrutiny for closure was that from York-Wakefield and Sowerby Bridge.

Yet another re-write of the West of England timetable came into force on May 5. Torbay services were separated from those to Plymouth eliminating the need to split trains at Newton Abbot, which allowed for a further reduction in end to end times. For a number of years the Cornish Riviera train had included in its title the word Express, but it reverted to its former name of Cornish Riviera Limited. ➤

A feature of the near derelict Birmingham Snow Hill was the display of posters that remained depicting past glories. Colour-Rail.com

Britain's Railways in the 1960s

The few remaining services between Rugby and Nottingham had been entrusted to DMUs since the closure of the rest of the route and a set is seen here at Rugby Central. All services were withdrawn on May 5. Colour-Rail.com

Trials took place at Longannet of the unloading apparatus needed to allow MGR trains to serve the power station there, these being worked by 8326/7. MGR services also served new power stations at Ironbridge and Didcot.

On August 4, 1969, a new freight service commenced between Cargo Fleet and Consett which conveyed molten metal in 'Torpedo Cars'. Each car had a gross weight of 240 tons and carried 100 tons of metal with a maximum permitted speed of 20mph.

The ending of passenger services between Manchester and Sheffield Victoria was agreed but it would not take place until January 3, 1970. Another line doomed to closure in the new year was Barnstaple-Ilfracombe

An illustration that British Rail was still not a 'joined up' organisation was that of services on Christmas day, where for instance, the Central section of the Southern Region did not provide any whilst an hourly service ran on LTS lines.

Observations

For visitors to the Isle of Wight a long time feature of Ryde Pier was the tramway service that operated alongside the trains. This was closed from January 27.

Despite only having been in use for around two years, carriages carrying blue and grey livery were being sold for scrap and much like many of the locomotives, had only been built in the 1950s. Indeed, the pace of the withdrawal of MK1 BR carriages accelerated quickly as requirements for air-braked stock increased. Despite this the use of pre nationalisation design catering vehicles in front line service continued, particularly those of LNER design.

An interesting development was the acquisition of a locomotive by the research department, this being D5705 which was renumbered S15705 and was to be used in adhesion experiments.

Having spent a considerable sum on point heaters to keep the points operating at times of snow and ice, where the points were manually, as opposed to electrically, operated problems still arose as the point rodding froze instead. Blizzards caused considerable disruption to services in the north of England in mid-February. Snow also affected the West country and blocked the Exeter-Plymouth route near

Both Manchester Exchange and Manchester Central stations were closed. The Central building, seen here, survived to become the G Mex conference centre and in 2020 during the Coronavirus pandemic became a Nightingale Hospital. Colour-Rail.com

1969

The Ryde Pier tram lies out of use in April after the service was withdrawn at the beginning of the year. David A Lawrence/Colour-Rail.com

Totnes. Despite the Okehampton route being officially closed, and with signalling removed, a freight service was sent via that route but also became stranded.

Earlier in the decade we noted the demise of the horsebox. However, on May 21 nearly 20 of them were included in a special train run to bring the Household Cavalry to Gorgie East in preparation for a visit by the Queen. But even this collection was over-shadowed on June 24, when in connection with the investiture of the Prince of Wales at Caernarvon, no fewer than 27 horseboxes were included in one train, making five more out and back trips to London up to July 4.

One headline incident of 1969 was when a 1000 ton ore train headed by 1617 ran out of control at Chester on July 9. In what was possibly not the wisest move, it was diverted into the loco shed where it collided with five Class 24 locos before coming to rest.

Western D1045 reached Derby on a service train on July 4, this being an extended Paddington-Cheltenham service put on due to a derailment in the West country. Hymeks 7046/58 penetrated as far as Lincoln in June on car trains.

A signalman's dispute in early July led to many cancellations and late running across the country. This formed just part of a trend towards outbreaks of such action, quite often unofficial and of short duration, but enough to dent public confidence in the railways.

Much regional shuffling of coaching stock took place in the year with the Scottish Region having to provide stock for all its internal services, whilst all services to/from England had stock provided by either the Eastern or Midland Region. The Western took on stock provision for services to Exeter via Salisbury.

In a red-letter day for enthusiasts, Derby Carriage and Wagon Works held an open day in August. Nearly 300 carriages were on site plus over 50 new vehicles under construction.

During the decade there had been a growth in special services for use by 'old people' to travel midweek to holiday destinations. They started life as being advertised for 'Old Age Pensioners' but by the end of the decade were called 'Senior Citizens' specials and were available to those over the age of 55.

The 27XXX class 77 electric locomotives were sold to Netherlands Railways but before shipment 27002 was used on a demonstration train for the purchasers from Reddish to Sheffield Victoria.

Some trains attracted attention of observers, one being the southbound Devonian from Bradford to Paignton. It had a notorious reputation for poor time keeping but recorded an on time arrival at Paignton on November 5, the first for six months.

And to demonstrate that what would make the news in 2020 also made headlines in 1969, the Daily Telegraph reported that Second Class passengers were to be banned from the restaurant car on the Liverpool-Birmingham-London route because they eat too slowly. It was alleged that their leisurely eating was preventing some First Class passengers from getting a meal.

A decade ending summary.

The decade ended with an ongoing theme of rationalisation and economy. Lines continued to be under threat and when closed the track was soon removed. Also shut down and cleared were locomotive servicing facilities but many country station sites were just abandoned to nature. Whilst research into new trains was underway, the existing fleet would soldier on for many years following the withdrawal of the various non-standard types. Blue and Grey would become all-pervading eventually and briefly the railway presented a fully corporate image.

Strangely, the public seemed to come to like steam trains and the heritage movement blossomed.

In the following pages we will look at few 1960s subjects in more detail.

Going back in time - Peak D93 climbs the Lickey incline with a steam banker at the head of the northbound Devonian. D93 was on loan to Bristol Bath Road for crew training at the time. T Owen/Colour-Rail.com

Britain's Railways in the 1960s

SAFETY

RAILWAY SAFETY IN THE 1960s

How safe is safe? Keeping safe is a relative term. In respect of the individual, if you personally were to be killed or injured the judgement would be that you had been involved in an unsafe act. On the other side of the coin, when running a vast operation like the railways it might be assumed that there was no way of avoiding the occasional injury or even death. In the 1960s therefore the railway industry could be deemed to have been relatively safe, as those travelling by rail had a lower probability of being killed than those using our roads or flying.

Over the course of the 1960s the average number of death/injury accidents on Britain's railways was 4.4 per year and deaths 18.7. The deaths figure was heavily influenced by the Hither Green and Hixon accidents mentioned earlier.

There is no evidence in the figures that the number of accidents per year was changing and possibly, other than when the two major accidents occurred, the view may well have been that there was not a great need to do better given the accident rates in other industries and modes of transport.

A freight train running away or failing to stop at the final signal in a goods loop could result in the train ending up at the bottom of an embankment as seen here with V2 60954 at Mirfield in 1962. Colour-Rail.com

THE FIGURES

The accident statistics for the years 1960-1969 make informative reading and are set out below

Year	Number of Accidents*	Number of Deaths
1960	3	11
1961	4	15
1962	2	21
1963	5	9
1964	6	10
1965	6	9
1966	1	2
1967	6	71
1968	6	24
1969	5	15

* Accidents in which an injury or death occurred

Slow speed incidents such as that involving newly delivered D418 at Preston were commonplace, track spreading or wrongly set points being the usual cause. Rather than getting cranes involved, the use of jacks might be all that was required to get the loco back on the tracks. G M Wilkinson/Colour-Rail.com

End of a Brush Type 4- although only one year old, D1734 was condemned following this accident at Coton Hill, Shrewsbury in January 1965. Colour-Rail.com

Recovery of a derailed engine could be challenging. When 48616 derailed at Turvey in July 1960 two cranes were needed to get it back on the rails. K Fairey/Colour-Rail.com

In that context it should be noted that as at the start of 2020 there had not been a rail passenger death as a result of a collision or derailment since 2007, the longest period on record since such an event. Sadly, in August 2020 a passenger's life, along with those of two train crew, was lost in the HST derailment near Stonehaven. Nonetheless things have certainly changed for the better in recent years.

As now, back in the 1960s all injury accidents were investigated, and recommendations made to prevent a recurrence. The three main causes of accidents were the misreading of signals, excessive speed and derailments. In respect of these it should be noted that in the 1960s not all trains were fitted with warning devices if a signal was not green, in the case of steam engines, many were not fitted with speedometers and for derailments it was found in a number of cases that a 'minor' derailment had occurred with the debris then hit by another train.

Having said that, the accuracy of reporting of injury information may also not be as good as it should have been. The author was involved in a rail accident not included in this analysis when his train was side swiped by a freight passing in the opposite direction, which contained derailed wagons. Some passengers required first aid but the incident does not appear in the list of injury accidents opposite, perhaps because they did not go to hospital. Also of note was the speed with which the whole incident was dealt with. The accident occurred just south of Pontypool Road with five out of ten carriages suffering damage. Both trains stopped, but within ten minutes the passenger train was underway again to its next booked stop at Pontypool Road. Within 15 minutes all the passengers from the damaged coaches were transferred to the front half of the train, the damaged coaches were detached and the train resumed its journey.

Carrying out research for this book it was evident that the railway scene was very different to that of today. There were derailments happening day in and day out, due in part to 'shunting mishaps' but more frequently to wagons in freight trains due to a combination of poor track and speed. This was a time, particularly in the early to mid-1960s that most goods trains were still composed of unbraked, short wheel base wagons. Having watched numerous freights in the day 'rattle past' and seeing the wagons bounce from side to side it would appear a miracle that the accident numbers were so low. ■

LAST OFF THE LINE
EVENING STAR

March 18, 1960 was marked with an official celebration and is remembered by many as a particularly poignant day – the day now over sixty years ago when the very last steam engine built for British Railways was named and became available for service at Swindon Works.

92220 *Evening Star* is one of the more famous of today's steam survivors and was even the subject of the £1m question on Who Wants to be a Millionaire. However, its survival was far from being a straightforward affair despite being designated for preservation from day one.

Of course, not numerically the last of the 251 9Fs, 92220 was the last to be completed. Sister locomotive 92250 had been put to traffic from Crewe works in December 1958. Swindon works did not put the first of the final batch 92203, into service until April 1959 and 92218/9 had the honour, along with 92220 of being new in 1960. The latter was completed in standard black livery in early February but was then held at the works pending the outcome of a naming competition and the decision to repaint it lined green topped off by a copper capped chimney. Its official entry into traffic date was March 25, 1960 and it was on BR's books for just five years and one day, being condemned on March 26, 1965.

Its first home was Cardiff Canton where it was very quickly rostered for a railtour when on April 3 it headed the LCGB Six Counties Limited from Paddington as far as Princes Risborough via Bourne End and later took the train to Yarnton.

Passenger duties quickly became the order of the day with its exploits on the Capitals United Express being well recorded in the railway press of the time before senior management got wind of what was going on and had 9Fs banned from front line work on the Western Region.

92220 stayed in South Wales until the summer of 1962 when, along with a small number of classmates it was selected to work from Bath Green Park on summer duties over the Somerset & Dorset route to Bournemouth. At the end of the season it moved briefly to Old Oak Common before reallocation to Oxford in October 1962. It returned late in the 1963 summer season to Bath where it famously worked the final Pines Express over the S&D in both directions lingering on the shed's book until October before returning to Cardiff but this time on the allocation of Cardiff East Dock as Canton shed was by now a diesel-only depot.

Late in 1964 it was discovered that *Evening Star's* nameplates had been stolen. The theft was thought to have been at Tyseley, although strangely this was not reported to the police until 1966! New plates were cast but in the event this proved to be a waste of money as the engine was involved in an accident at Pontypool Road leading to its condemnation in March 1965.

At this point it might be expected that the engine would be taken into the care of the national collection but the curator of historical relics refused to take it in damaged condition with repair costs being quoted of £1,029 which the general manager of the Western Region also refused to pay for. In an effort to circumvent the situation the engine was offered to Swindon Corporation but the offer was declined. A sale was then pursued, initially with a Mr Snowden at an asking price of £4,000 but funds were not forthcoming. During this time the engine was in open storage but following interest from a Mr Green it was moved to Crewe works for inspection in November 1966.

It seems that rampant inflation was involved as the purchase cost including a repair was now put at £14,000. Negotiations with this person dragged on and somewhere along the line Crewe works undertook a complete restoration and repaint at an estimated cost of £10,000.

In January 1968, the engine was moved to the former Pullman works at Brighton. A year later Mr Green was apparently still interested and carried out further inspections, one of which revealed that rust was to be seen. This led to a further dispute concerning responsibility for rectification. As Mr Green was believed to be procrastinating, the purchase

92220 at its naming ceremony in Swindon works. It was originally painted in standard black but once selected for special attention gained lined green livery complete with a copper-capped chimney. Colour-Rail.com

There must have been a change of heart in top management as the engine was specifically selected to work the final Pines Express over Somerset & Dorset metals in September 1962 and it is seen here on Bath Green Park shed the day after the final run. Colour-Rail.com

Britain's Railways in the 1960s

92220 was quickly put to work on passenger duties including on named trains such as the Capitals United Express and is seen here at Newport in July 1960. However, its exploits soon became known to senior management who demanded its removal from high profile work. Colour-Rail.com

92220 undergoing restoration at Crewe on June 18, 1967. D Preston/Colour-Rail.com

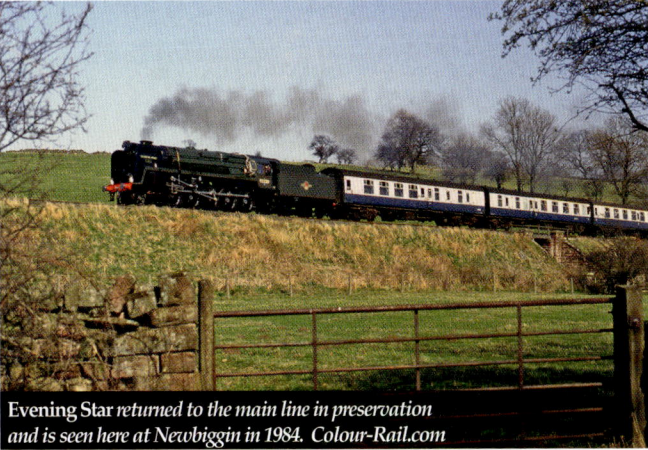

Evening Star returned to the main line in preservation and is seen here at Newbiggin in 1984. Colour-Rail.com

options for a sale to the USA were investigated going even to the point of considering getting an engine out of Barry docks to replace 92220 in the national collection. Eventually the Department of Education & Science intervened bringing to bear Section 144 (7) of the Transport act of 1968 which stipulated that the BR Board could not dispose of the engine without first offering it to them. The upshot of all the wrangling was that the engine survived long enough to be taken into the national collection. Thus, it appeared in the public gaze for the first time in several years when it took part in the Stockton & Darlington celebrations in August 1975. The following year saw it run some main line tours before being sidelined with a cracked cylinder. This occurred at about the same time that BR decreed that as it had a flangeless centre driving wheels, which it was believed could foul raised check rails and lead to derailment, the locomotive could not operate on the national system. A policy change saw it re-emerge in 1980 for the Rainhill celebrations and it was used on some railtours.

In 1981 it was retubed and repainted at Didcot and then carried out railtour work which for the most part saw it working in the north of England although in April 1986 it worked an Edinburgh-Gleneagles duty. *Evening Star's* last recorded main line duties were in August 1988 and following a summer season on the West Somerset Railway in 1989 it retired to York with, it would seem, little chance of ever returning to mainline action, at least over Network Rail lines due to the centre wheel flange issue. ■

Britain's Railways in the 1960s

SPOTTERS

SPOTTERS, CLUBS AND RAILTOURS

The railways of Britain had always attracted the attention of enthusiasts and their younger version, the train spotter. The collecting bug is something that many people have, and in this case, it was the collecting of engine numbers that was the driving force of the interest in railways. The 1950s and 1960s saw the peak of the hobby probably driven by three factors, the baby boom, Ian Allan ABC publications and the demise of steam power. The Ian Allan ABCs became widely available after the war and with the nationalisation of the railways the whole fleet of engines could be listed without number duplication.

Critically the books were priced to be affordable by the saving of a few weeks' pocket money. The fact that there were many thousands of youngsters in the mid-1950s onwards, all looking for something to do with their spare time, saw train spotting become THE thing to do. Ian Allan had its own spotters club and at one time membership exceeded 100,000. With the realisation that the steam engine was in decline, many spotters concentrated on tracking down their last 'wants' wherever they might be in the country and their older brethren chose to travel over lines that were about to be closed.

Spotters were everywhere and crowded some stations to the point that they were banned because there were too many. One place where this could be seen was at Tamworth, at the point where the West Coast mainline crossed the Midland route from the north to the southwest. On a busy day, a convenient field adjacent to the station could be filled with hundreds of spotters.

As well as inhabiting the stations, spotters would congregate around engine sheds and of course seek ways in to collect the numbers of the engines lurking within the shed itself. The fact that they should have a permit did not deter the majority and legion are the tales of being ejected from the premises by the shed foreman.

The desire to carry out such visits and to travel to more distant sheds spawned the formation of many railway clubs and societies. Some such as the Railway Correspondence and Travel Society and the Stephenson Locomotive Society had been running for many years and as well as providing the opportunity to join shed visits also had house magazines and organised meetings, but other groups existed solely to run shed trips, both with and without the required permits! Whilst some societies tried to use rail travel to get to the distant sheds it was more usual to hire a coach and it was not long before first overnight trips and then weekend 'bashes' became common, with some Scottish outings taking up to four days over the Easter holidays.

Particularly towards the end of steam, some classes of engine such as Jubilees had large groups of followers and every movement would be followed whilst service trains that employed them would be packed with enthusiasts.

Line closures and 'last of class' events led to an explosion in the number of enthusiasts railtours that were run, most organised by a relatively small number of the larger societies.

They utilised everything from a few goods brakevans, through push-pull sets to multi engine events that took engines to places where they had never been seen before.

A joint RCTS and SLS railtour of Scotland ran for ten days and visited much of the country including freight- only lines.

The web site www.sixbellsjunction.co.uk records around 55 railtours run in 1960. By 1964 that many were running in a three month period, but by 1969 activity was back to 1960 levels. However, by then most trips were worked by a DMU or *Flying Scotsman*.

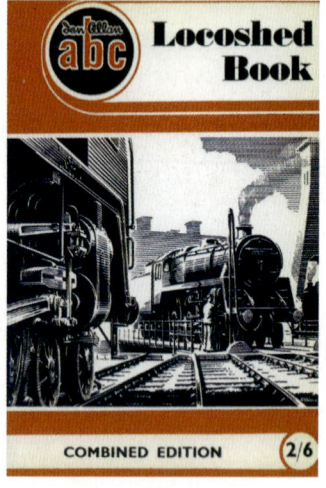

Early editions of Ian Allan ABC books had covers illustrated with line drawings as here, but later photographs were used. Colour-Rail.com

Jubilee worship at Carlisle. July 10, 1965. D Forsyth/Colour-Rail.com

Railtours took all forms and this one, which involved visiting freight lines around Widnes, used goods brakevans to transport the passengers on August 5, 1967. Colour-Rail.com

Despite their relatively young age, most spotters could be relied upon to behave and were even trusted in locations where there was no fencing. School blazers and often caps were the accepted dress for a day at the lineside. Colour-Rail.com

Britain's Railways in the 1960s

NAMING
NAMED TRAINS

In the 1960s there was a plethora of named trains, possibly more than at any time in the history of our railways. World War Two had seen the titled train disappear but the process of reviving our railways and speeding up trains thereafter warranted denoting the primary express trains on each route and the best way to do that was to give them each titles. Going full circle, the advent of even interval timetables, stock efficiencies, the spread of the use of DMUs and the corporate image imposed at the end of steam saw the named train once again go into decline. The photographs that follow are a celebration of the 1960s named train.

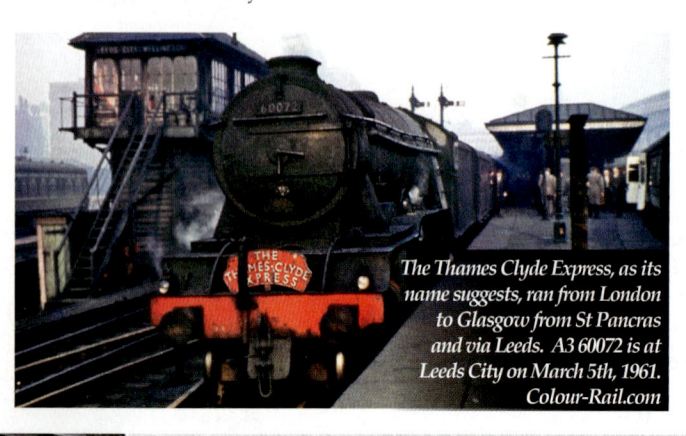

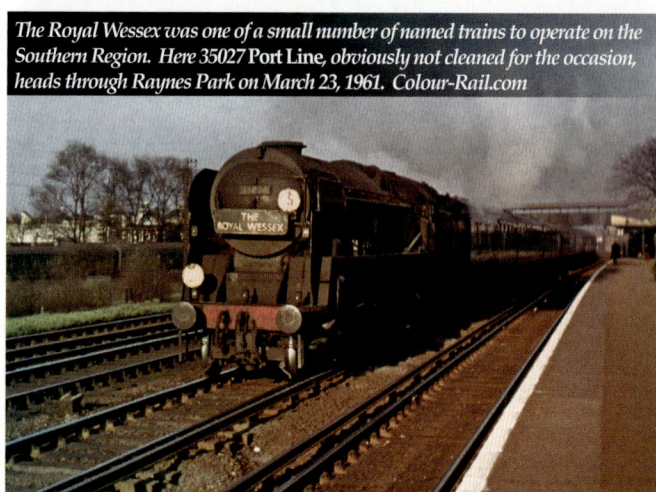

The most famous train on the West Coast route was the Royal Scot which is seen here with 46242 City of Glasgow *rushing through Lichfield on April 23, 1960. Colour-Rail.com*

The Thames Clyde Express, as its name suggests, ran from London to Glasgow from St Pancras and via Leeds. A3 60072 is at Leeds City on March 5th, 1961. Colour-Rail.com

The Royal Wessex was one of a small number of named trains to operate on the Southern Region. Here 35027 Port Line, *obviously not cleaned for the occasion, heads through Raynes Park on March 23, 1961. Colour-Rail.com*

Britain's Railways in the 1960s

Cardiff Canton briefly had an allocation of Kings and here 6019 King Henry V uses Goring troughs to advantage on its way to London with The Red Dragon on March 4, 1961. T Owen/Colour-Rail.com

An early change from steam to diesel power was seen on the East Coast route with the Talisman being one of the first conversions. D243 comes through Grantham on June 20, 1960. D Ovenden/Colour-Rail.com

Not every named train was hauled by an express passenger engine, nor was it long or formed of the latest rolling stock. Ivatt 2MT works The Welsh Dragon on July 1, 1962. Colour-Rail.com

One of the few cross country named trains was The Cornishman running from Wolverhampton through to Penzance. Here North British Type 2 D6304 and Castle 4087 are about to tackle Dainton bank. Colour-Rail.com

Two for the price of one at Euston as Royal Scot 46111 on The Mancunian and D215 on The Merseyside Express stand side by side at Euston. M J Reade/Colour-Rail.com

The Orcadian had a brief career, only operating from 1962-1964 between Inverness and Wick and is seen here waiting to depart from the former. Colour-Rail.com

The Golden Hind was a product of the modern traction age in that it was introduced in 1964 as part of an improved service from the West Country to London. A headboard was never carried. D1036 is seen near Twyford on July 26, 1969. T Owen/Colour-Rail

One of the few named trains operating from Liverpool Street was The Day Continental and often attracted only mixed traffic motive power, in this case B1 61372 in April 1960. Colour-Rail.com

PULLMANS

PULLMAN TRAINS AND CAMPING COACHES

On the railways the term Pullman was, and still is to some extent, synonymous with luxury travel. The Pullman Company originated in the United States of America and came to this country in 1874 when the first carriage was included in a train from Bradford to St Pancras. The Pullman Car Company was founded here in 1882 and had a workshop at Brighton although Pullman carriages, or cars as they were always called, were built elsewhere in the UK as well.

The first complete train of Pullmans was run by the London Brighton and South Coast Railway. The livery of Umber Brown and cream was adopted, and the practice of First Class cars being named whilst Second Class cars carried numbers evolved. The Pullman Car Company continued as a privately owned enterprise until 1962 before being taken over by British Railways. Following the takeover, the Pullman works at Brighton was closed in 1964.

Whilst Pullman services had operated on a number of routes across the country, 1960 saw the majority of trains operating on the East Coast mainline into Kings Cross plus the Bournemouth Belle, Golden Arrow and the only electric service, the Brighton Belle, running on the Southern along with the South Wales Pullman on the Western Region.

However, things were about to change, as early in 1960 the first sightings of new diesel Pullman units were reported, these being in a striking new livery of Nanking Blue and white. Two six-car sets were for use from St Pancras to Manchester whilst eight-car sets were to run on the Western Region from Paddington to Bristol and Birmingham. One of the Midland sets was at Marylebone station for inspection on May 29 and a demonstration run took place to High Wycombe from there on June 23. The Western Region services were launched on September 12 with two return trips on each route, although that on the Bristol service was noted as taking five minutes longer than the Bristolian.

The traditional locomotive-hauled trains, in addition to those mentioned above, were on the East Coast route and in 1960 comprised the Master Cutler (a recent introduction as a Pullman train) from Sheffield, the Harrogate Sunday Pullman that actually reached as far as Newcastle, the Queen of Scots which ran to both Edinburgh and Glasgow, the Yorkshire Pullman and the long running Tees Tyne Pullman.

The Eastern services varied a little through the decade. The Master Cutler lasted until 1966 and upon its withdrawal led to protests that Sheffield was the only major city not to have a Pullman ➤

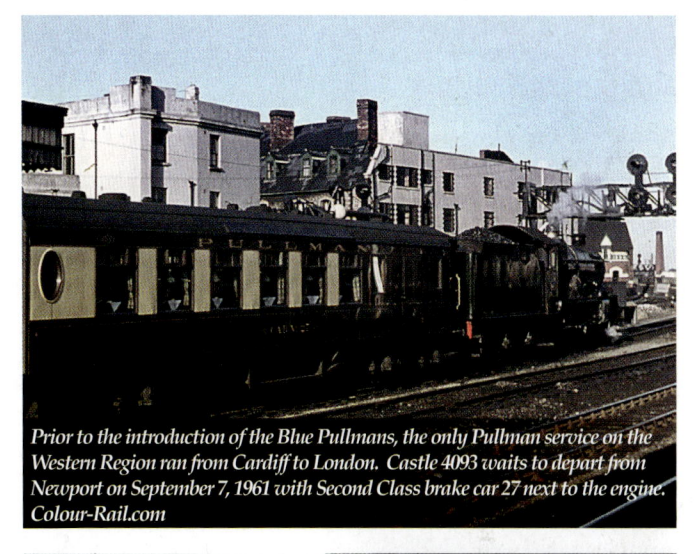

Prior to the introduction of the Blue Pullmans, the only Pullman service on the Western Region ran from Cardiff to London. Castle 4093 waits to depart from Newport on September 7, 1961 with Second Class brake car 27 next to the engine. Colour-Rail.com

Unusual power for a Pullman was N15 tank 69153 which is banking the Queen of Scots service out of Glasgow Queen Street in May 1961. Colour-Rail.com

September 12, 1960 saw the arrival at Paddington of the first diesel Pullman sets from both Bristol and Birmingham. Colour-Rail.com

Britain's Railways in the 1960s 87

The 5 BEL EMUs used on the Brighton Belle Service succumbed to BR blue and grey as seen here at London Bridge in 1969. However, all other Pullman cars had the livery reversed and were thus mainly light grey with blue window surrounds. Colour-Rail.com

service to London. The Queen of Scots ceased in 1964 at which time a new service, the White Rose to Leeds started. This ran until 1967. There were also Yorkshire and Hull Pullman services from 1967 and The Talisman briefly had a Pullman portion. The Tees Tyne service ran throughout the decade.

On the Southern Region the Bournemouth Belle ceased in 1967 when the full Bournemouth line electrification went live, whilst the Golden Arrow and Brighton Belle continued. The Brighton Belle was unique in having its own dedicated electric stock being three 5 BEL units with two being required in traffic at any time. These acquired the new blue and grey colour scheme with the first, 3052, being noted in December 1968.

The Southern also operated six-carriage electric units which included a single Pullman car, which stood out in its brown and cream livery for the rest of the set designated 6 PUL, which were painted green.

On the Midland the new service from St Pancras ran until 1966 at which time it was replaced by new trains composed of upgraded standard design carriages running from Euston to both Manchester and Liverpool and electrically hauled from the outset. The two Midland diesel sets then transferred to the Western Region.

On the Western the South Wales Pullman was formed initially of conventional Pullman stock but in due course was diagrammed for a diesel set. The arrival of the Midland sets and the withdrawal of the Birmingham route trains, on completion of the West Coast electrification, allowed the Western to start running services to Oxford. Both the diesel sets, and the locomotive-hauled stock lost the famous brown and cream colours for the 'reverse' grey and blue paint scheme.

Those using the Pullman services had to pay a supplement on top of the standard First or Second Class fare.

Given the reputation of some football supporters of the period, it was perhaps surprising to see the diesel Pullman sets employed on football excursions from time to time, which also saw them work far from home on occasions with for instance one set appearing at Hartlepool in 1965. They were also used on some race meeting specials.

So, what is the connection with the subject of Camping Coaches? It seems that the first camping coaches appeared in 1933 and in due course were to be found at over 150 locations across the country. The accommodation was usually provided in stock that was already past its sell by date. World War Two saw the service suspended but coaches were re-instated from 1952, usually located in goods yards or sidings on branch lines as the usual locations were either seaside or rural in nature.

The 1960s demanded something a little more up market and a number of older Pullman carriages, which had been replaced by more modern stock on the main line, joined the camping coach fleet which, in 1962 stood at over 200 vehicles. Thereafter numbers declined, in part due to many of the sites being on lines that were closed as loss making. ■

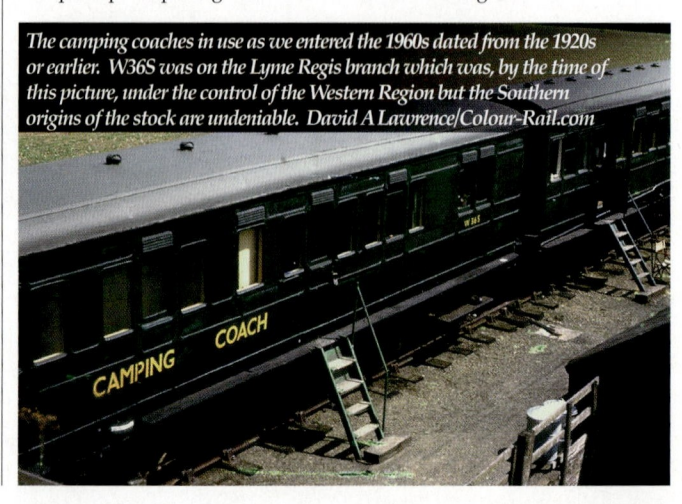

The Sheffield Pullman was hauled almost exclusively by diesel power from the outset and here Type 2 D5688 heads the train past Wymondly. Colour-Rail.com

Pullman cars were noted for their plush interiors as seen here within the Brighton Belle set. Colour-Rail.com

The camping coaches in use as we entered the 1960s dated from the 1920s or earlier. W36S was on the Lyme Regis branch which was, by the time of this picture, under the control of the Western Region but the Southern origins of the stock are undeniable. David A Lawrence/Colour-Rail.com

Britain's Railways in the 1960s

THE S&D

The final breath of the Somerset and Dorset as 48706 and 80043 stand at the buffer stop at Bath Green Park having worked the final northbound special. March 6, 1966. T Owen/Colour-Rail.com

THE SOMERSET & DORSET JOINT RAILWAY

Certain railway lines were looked on with some affection, if that is the right term, by the enthusiasts and the public that used them. One that closed before the Beeching era was the large Midland & Great Northern system in Lincolnshire. Others that come to mind were the Settle and Carlisle route, the Great Central, the Waverley line and the Somerset and Dorset, always known as the 'S&D'. Its fascination has perhaps grown since closure as it has been immortalised in books primarily featuring the photography of one man, Ivo Peters, who spent many hours recording its fading years.

Its nature as a 'joint railway' was perhaps the key to its interest, as it was run by both the Midland and Southern railways but penetrated the heart of Great Western territory. The fact that until well after nationalisation most of the motive power was of LMS origin and that it had its own unique class, the 7F 2-8-0s, made it stand out in southern England. Visiting engines pressed into service could mean locomotives from the northwest and Yorkshire sheds were seen on the south coast. Added to the mix, on busy summer Saturdays Bulleid Pacifics were to be seen and double heading was the norm between Bath and Evercreech Junction.

Control of much of the line passed to the Western Region in 1958, which in due course was to ensure that the line died. However, in the short term the change just increased the diversity of engines employed, as BR Standard types gradually replaced former LMS power, but the same chance of borrowed engines from almost anywhere on the Midland remained. Indeed, at Bath itself Eastern Region B1s also appeared. The final addition to the mix were some GW types such as the 2251 class and the ubiquitous pannier tanks. Diesel power rarely appeared and then not beyond Bath Green Park. The line was known for its one named train, the Pines Express, and for most of the year it was one of the few through trains. It was summer Saturdays when the line came alive with capacity used to the full and there would be a procession of holiday trains. The fact that the 7Fs were pressed into service on these duties enhanced the appeal of the line.

As mentioned previously, many trains needed to be double headed over the tortuous northern section of the line where it climbed the Mendip hills and it was not until 1960 that a solution to this appeared. That came in the shape of the 9F 2-10-0 which proved capable of handling almost any load over the route. However, it was not enough to save the line and in 1962 the final Pines Express, and the other through trains, made their way over the Mendips. Thereafter it saw the Western Region management do all that it could to make the case for closure by providing a minimal service at inconvenient times. Despite that the spirit of the close knit group of staff who worked the line could not be dented. The end was supposed to come on January 3, 1966 but last minute problems with arranging a replacement bus service ensured another two months of dying agony was inflicted on the line with services further reduced on the pretence that insufficient serviceable motive power was available to provide any more.

The final curtain came down on a dark March night as high up on the Mendips two specials passed each other, one hauled by a pair of Bulleid Pacifics and the other by an 8F and a BR Standard tank. ■

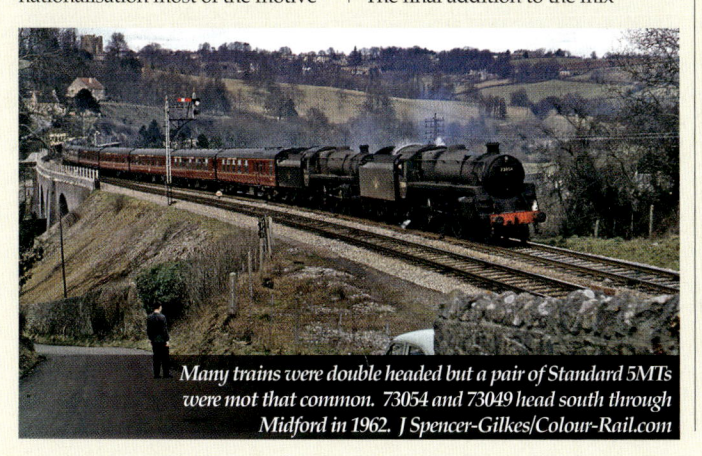

Many trains were double headed but a pair of Standard 5MTs were mot that common. 73054 and 73049 head south through Midford in 1962. J Spencer-Gilkes/Colour-Rail.com

53801 bursts out of Chilcompton tunnel with the Exmouth-Cleethorpes Saturday-only train, one of the few that did not require double heading across the Mendips. T Owen/Colour-Rail.com

Britain's Railways in the 1960s

SCRAP

SCRAP YARDS

It is an unavoidable fact of life that most of what we use and consume will one day end up on the scrap heap, be that the local council tip or a place where the raw materials are recovered and reused. Railway locomotives and carriages had long since fallen into the recycling category as any metal components could be recovered and either reused directly or melted down to form parts of another generation of motive power. Traditionally the railway had carried out the scrapping process at the main works with engines arriving and being assessed for repair or dismantling.

Spotters of the day who had a permit to visit a railway workshop were usually allowed to amble up and down the scrap roads and in the early days no doubt collected the odd souvenir along the way. Two things changed as the 1960s grew to a close. Firstly, the railways started storing considerable numbers of locomotives, often at sites away from sheds, no doubt as insurance against the mass failure of new diesels, but also in case of a sudden upturn in demand. And secondly, the sheer number of engines being withdrawn led to a situation where the works cutting facilities simply could not keep pace with the rate of withdrawals.

Once the decision to also withdraw much of the stored stock was taken, workshops were simply overwhelmed, and vast numbers of locomotives were sold to contractors for breaking. Many of the breakers were in areas associated with steel making and heavy industry resulting in engines having to be towed long distances for scrapping with many ending up in areas where the types had never been seen before such as GWR types in East Anglia and Southern engines widely distributed across South Wales. Eventually all the BR workshops ceased cutting up altogether, with Eastleigh possibly being the last to be active. Thus, when it came to modern traction types being scrapped many of them also went to scrap merchants.

Some yards would deconstruct an engine within hours of its arrival whilst others would leave them to languish for weeks, months or in the case of Barry docks, years. The latter allowed more than 200 to survive which ultimately formed the basis of the large heritage fleet we see today.

Another engine to survive its trip to the scrap yard was Stanier 5MT 45305, which was consigned to Drapers at Hull, who had broken up many engines but 45305 was among the last to arrive and the owners decided that it should be saved for posterity.

Some enthusiasts used to enjoy going to scrap yards, some to cop engines that they had missed in service and others to look for souvenirs. Some were greeted with 'what would you like to see or buy', others with a number of very wild looking Alsatians! ■

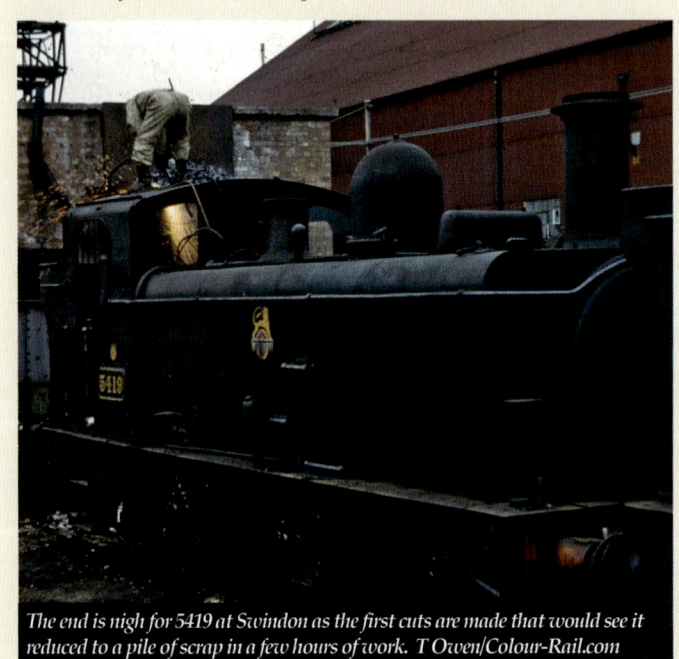

The end is nigh for 5419 at Swindon as the first cuts are made that would see it reduced to a pile of scrap in a few hours of work. T Owen/Colour-Rail.com

Stored engines as far as the eye can see at Over and Wharton. P Hughes/Colour-Rail

Baby Deltic D5900 met its end at Cransley in Northamptonshire, with what was left of it being photographed in July 1969. K Fairey/Colour-Rail.com

Back from the grave. Stanier 5MT 45305 was saved from cutting up by the scrap merchant that had bought it, Drapers of Hull. In due course it returned to the mainline. It is seen here at Horton in Ribblesdale in 1980. Colour-Rail.com

Britain's Railways in the 1960s

TIME CAPSULE

THE ISLE OF WIGHT TIME CAPSULE

The first railway on the Isle of Wight opened in 1862, linking Cowes and Newport. It was followed in 1864 by the line from Ryde to Shanklin and the route to Ventnor opened just two years later. A further line was that from Ryde to Newport which diverged from the Shanklin line at Smallbrook Junction. Further lines ran to Ventnor Town and Freshwater plus the eventual extension of services on to Ryde Pier.

The island's railways became the property of the London and South Western Railway immediately before that company became part of the Southern Railway. Thereafter the Southern became responsible for both the motive power and rolling stock and over time transferred already old versions of both to the Island with, in the end, the O2 0-4-4 tanks forming most of the motive power.

Nationalisation essentially passed the island system by, as only the colour of the paint applied to the locomotives and some carriages changed, to the point that the system became almost a living museum.

The future of the lines came increasingly into question, especially after the Beeching report emerged which sought to close the whole system. No doubt because of its isolation and the fact that BR thought the problem would ➤

The end of BR steam was recorded not just by photographers but by renowned artist David Shepherd, seen here capturing the scene at Ryde shed. At the time of writing, the original being created here is on sale at the David Shepherd Wildlife Foundation. Colour-Rail.com

Britain's Railways in the 1960s

91

The curtain came down on BR steam on the island at the end of December 1966 and a partly cleaned 14 officiates on the last day. Colour-Rail.com

The former London Transport tube stock that came to the island was at best over 30 years old and it was to see use for well over a further 20 years. Set 042 is seen here at Ryde. Colour-Rail.com

go away via closure, no plans had been in place to upgrade or replace the engines or carriages. When it became evident that a solution was probably going to be required an idea that had been aired a couple of years earlier re-emerged and started to be acted upon, this being to send a number of BR Standard 2MT tanks to the island, and 84010/3-7/9/25/6/8 were transferred from the Midland to the Southern for this project.

Ultimately, only 84014 travelled south to Eastleigh and had not even entered the works before the plan was abandoned.

Eventually the use of former London Transport tube stock was agreed and indeed some stock was in store on the Southern for possible use at around the time the 84XXX tanks had been transferred. Eventually only Ryde to Shanklin was saved, with the line to Cowes having closed in February 1966 and that to Ventnor in April, whilst Ryde Pier Head closed on September 18.

The 1960s opened with just one of four E1 tanks left active and this only lasted until November of that year. Thereafter the O2 tanks reigned supreme. 15, 19, 23 and 34 had fallen by the wayside in the 1950s. Engine 25 was condemned in December 1962, 18, 30, 32 and 36 went in 1964 or 1965, but the rest of the fleet survived into the final year of steam services.

As noted earlier, 24 and 31 were retained until March 1967 to help with engineering work and were accompanied by the first diesel to work on the island - D2554 - which had arrived on October 7, 1967. Electric services began in March 1967 using stock built between 1924 and 1934. Then 1971 would see the birth of a heritage railway on the island with a genuine local engine at its heart, O2 24 *Calbourne*. ■

Britain's Railways in the 1960s

DELTICS

THE DELTICS

Some modern traction locomotive classes attracted attention even in the 1960s when steam was still prevalent. Unsurprisingly it was the Deltics that were at the top of the pile, being the most powerful diesel locomotives on the system and always associated with the most prestigious services on the East Coast mainline.

However, we start the story back in 1955 when the prototype Deltic entered service, the building of this 3,300hp locomotive being entirely the result of a private initiative by English Electric. At the time of its introduction it had no competitors other than steam power, as only 10000/1 and 10201-3 were in use on passenger duties, and these were far less powerful than Deltic. In its blue livery and looking very American in outline, it was bound to attract attention. The 1955 modernisation plan ordered several prototype diesels for evaluation but nothing larger than a 2,000 hp unit was included.

In the following years Deltic spent time on both the west and east coast routes. Initially it had been suggested that both lines might be electrified but the east coast route was quickly dropped from the proposals and the minds of management, who had been used to running trains at high speed with the A4 Pacifics, looked for a suitable replacement which they did not see among the various new classes then being constructed.

An order for 22 Deltic class diesels was placed, to be numbered D9000-21 with the intention that as a minimum they would replace all the A4s and allow most services between Kings Cross and the north to be Deltic-hauled.

Delivery of the first members of the class was expected in 1960 but it was in fact January 1961 when D9001 was taken into stock and March 1962 before the whole class was available for work. They were allocated only to Finsbury ➤

The prototype Deltic prepares to depart from Kings Cross on The White Rose. Colour-Rail.com

D9000 as delivered at Haymarket in 1961 having neither yellow warning panels nor a name. Colour-Rail.com

Britain's Railways in the 1960s

93

Park, Gateshead and Haymarket and were maintained at Doncaster works. The intention was that the initial allocations be maintained and this manifested itself in the naming of the engines, with those at Finsbury Park soon receiving the names of racehorses, no Deltic being named at the time of delivery. Indeed, it was to be May 1965 before D9010 was named. Those at Gateshead and Haymarket received regimental names appropriate to the area.

Unlike the prototype the engines had to carry the standard BR green, although this was offset by having a lighter green band at the bottom of the body. In due course they acquired the yellow high visibility panel followed by BR blue with full yellow ends and finally in the 1960s the removal of the D prefix.

They were also fitted with air brakes in the blue era which saw a temporary reallocation of the fleet.

Because of their high profile, every move of the class was recorded initially, especially when they failed to materialise for a high speed duty, usually being substituted in the early days by an A4 and it took around two years for them to realise their full potential day in and out. Journey times were progressively trimmed as stretches of line where the full potential of their 100mph top speed could be realised. Much like the A4 chime whistle, the engine noise of a Deltic distinguished them from the rest of the fleet, especially when under the overall roofs of the major stations on the line. In the 1960s they rarely strayed from the East Coast route but D9007 was used on a farewell to the Waverley Route railtour on January 5, 1969. ■

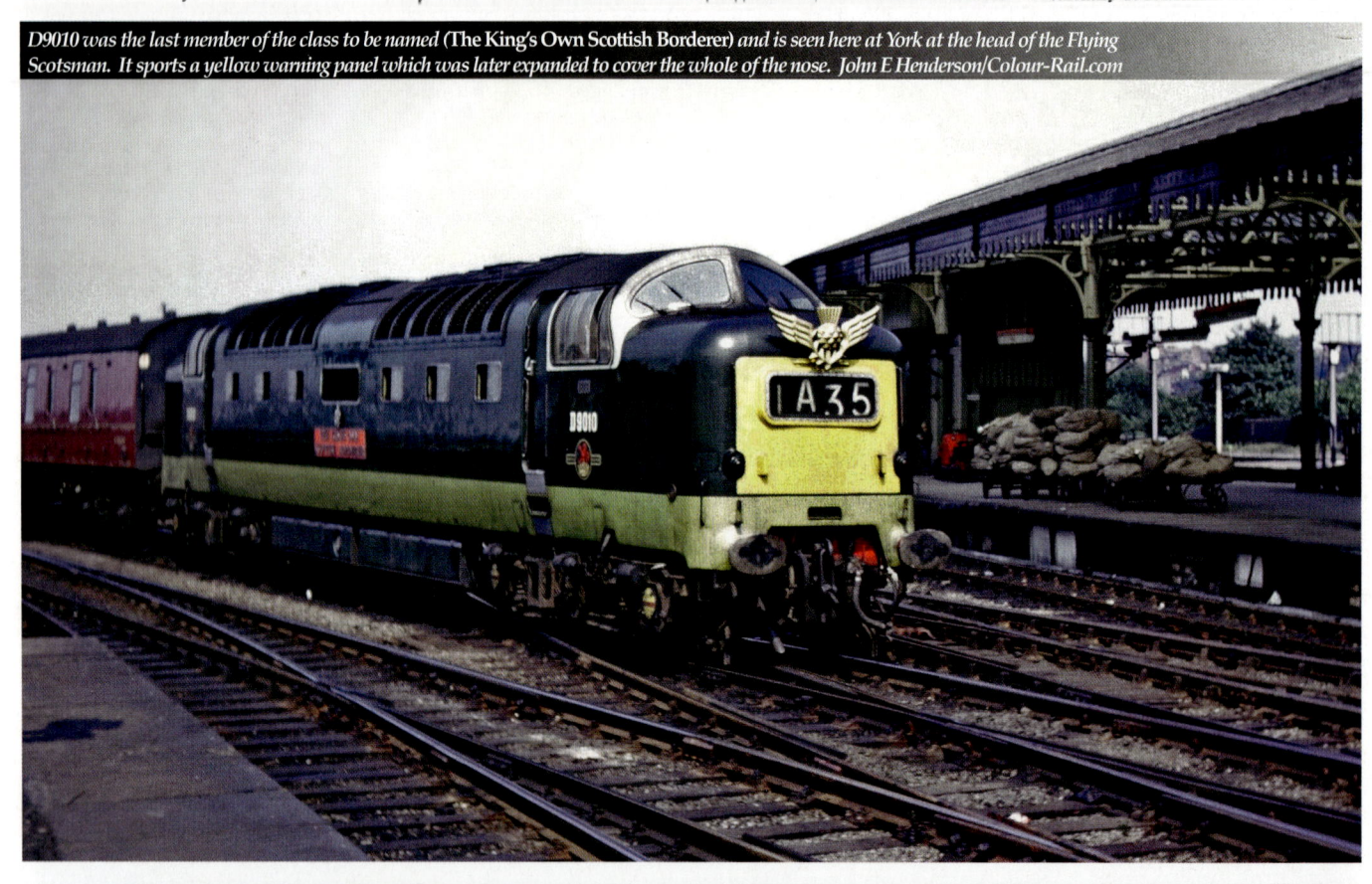

D9010 was the last member of the class to be named (**The King's Own Scottish Borderer**) *and is seen here at York at the head of the Flying Scotsman. It sports a yellow warning panel which was later expanded to cover the whole of the nose. John E Henderson/Colour-Rail.com*

At the time, D9007 **Pinza** *was an unusual choice for working a railtour, but it officiated on the RCTS tour to mark the closing of the Waverley route. It is seen at Riccarton Junction on January 5, 1969. Colour-Rail.com*

PRESERVATION

PRESERVATION AND HERITAGE

The saving of items of engineering from the scrap heap to illustrate the technological growth of the country fortunately seemed to be a trait of the British, particularly when applied to the railways. Artefacts of all sizes, including locomotives, were rescued primarily by those who had used them or by museums, so that everything from *Rocket* and *Locomotion* through to the Stirling single were there for all to see, although nearly all were non-operational being on static display at a location relevant to their use. In 1927 the LNER alone had seen fit to provide a museum to house some of its engines, this being located at York and in due course it provided a home for engines from some other railways such as *Gladstone* from the London Brighton and South Coast Railway.

A list of locomotives that fully illustrated the later history of our railways was drawn up in the British Railways era and these were duly put to one side as they were withdrawn. However, nowhere had been put aside for their restoration and display. The Transport Museum, based in a former London Transport garage at Clapham opened its doors in 1960, although larger exhibits could not be accommodated immediately and it did not have anywhere near enough room to take all the locomotives on the preservation list although pride of place was given to A4 *Mallard* upon its retirement.

In 1961 the Science Museum had given 4073 *Caerphilly Castle* a home and a Great Western Museum was opened in a former church building in Swindon in 1962. This housed Dean Goods 2516, 3440 *City of Truro*, 4003 *Lode Star* and 0-6-0PT 9400.

Most of the rest of the items for the collection were hidden away from public view and were gradually gathered at the disused works at Stratford, East London. Following the closure of the Pullman works at Preston Park Brighton, the Stratford engines then moved there. However, it was not until the establishment of the National Railway Museum at ➤

A view inside the old museum at York showed its cramped and traditional nature. J Sutton/Colour-Rail.com

The museum at Clapham opened its doors in 1960 and would remain until the opening of the new museum at York. Colour-Rail.com

Britain's Railways in the 1960s

95

4003 Lode Star is manoeuvred into the museum at Swindon. T Owen/Colour-Rail.com

York in the 1970s that the collection could be brought mostly under one roof and made suitable for public display.

In the 1960s it was never considered that the exhibits might ever turn a wheel in steam again, except for a small number of the national collection that were housed in a new, privately run museum at Bressingham in Norfolk. This became the home of 70013 *Oliver Cromwell* amongst others, and the site had a short demonstration line alongside the museum building.

Purchases and donations saw other engines saved from the scrap yard but again they were almost all for static display. Butlins holiday camps had LMS engines and Terrier 0-6-0 tanks. Some were sent to the United States such as A4 60008 whilst another A4, 60010 went to Canada.

However good the official schemes were in preserving our heritage they were no substitute for steam in action but the only way that was going to happen was for private individuals to get involved.

The concept of preservation and operation of a railway by enthusiasts started in this country in 1951 with the running of trains on the Talyllyn Railway. Whilst all the challenges were the same regardless of the track gauge, the running of narrow gauge lines was seen to be a possibility as the size and general complexity of everything was more feasible to handle and the Talyllyn was followed by the Ffestiniog Railway in 1955.

Before progressing to the next part of the story it is important to note the two separate threads that were to emerge. Many preservation groups were formed in the coming years, but the majority were concerned primarily about saving a locomotive. Where to put it was a secondary thought and often not really considered until the loco purchase was confirmed. The other strand to preservation was of those groups who set out to save a line, possibly with no locomotive to run on it. The two managed to evolve alongside each other but initially many rescued locomotives were kept in entirely unsuitable places, usually a very short siding or yard with no cover whatsoever to carry out repair and restoration work.

It is not proposed to give a comprehensive view of what has in recent times become known as heritage railways but to paint a broad picture of 1960s activities.

Besides the afore mentioned 'locos dumped in sidings' a small number of mainly express passenger locomotives were saved with the specific intention of running them on British Railways lines. The most high-profile of all of course was 60103 *Flying Scotsman*, bought by Alan Pegler

The privately owned museum at Bressingham housed several exhibits from the national collection including 70013 Oliver Cromwell. Colour-rail.com

The restarted Talyllyn Railway had already been open for 15 years when this picture was taken in 1966. Colour-Rail.com

4472 Flying Scotsman saw frequent use on specials before being shipped to the United States at the end of 1969. In preparation for its tour it acquired a second tender, bell, and a new whistle with one of its last duties being this tour on August 31. Colour-Rail.com

and following a repaint and refurbishment was soon back in action across the network. He had the foresight to conclude a running agreement with British Railways that, in the event, allowed the engine to operate beyond the end of BR steam when all other network steam activity was banned.

Other main line performers were A4s 60009/19 and Castles 4079 and 7029 but also 3442 *The Great Marquess*. Less well known was J52 1247. All these engines were left 'looking for a home' when British Railways imposed its steam ban.

While there were countless appeals to buy engines directly from British Railways, many fell by the wayside as the money could not be raised in the time between withdrawal and the engine being sold for scrap. However, a number were indeed saved. Particularly in the early years these were small engines, mainly tanks, as people assessed a) what they could afford and b) what they could maintain and run. Other than 46201 *Princess Elizabeth* few large engines were saved until the final cull in 1968 which saw larger engines such as Stanier Black 5s and 2-6-4 tanks rescued, mainly with a potential use and home identified. Nearly all the larger engines that we see today came via Woodhams scrap yard in Barry, South Wales. Even saving those saw a BR decision reversed, as when sold initially there was a clause in the contract that specified that they were for scrap only. 0-6-0 43924 was the first engine to leave Barry for preservation and by the end of 1969 those already removed or purchased and waiting a new home was approaching double figures.

Returning to the start of the decade we then come to the groups whose primary aim was to preserve a railway line or facility. Both the Middleton Railway in Leeds and the Bluebell Railway lay claim to operating the first standard gauge passenger services. The Middleton was a former industrial line which had not carried the public before, whilst the Bluebell was the first former BR line to have its services restored by a preservation group. Much could be written about the saving of that line and the acquisition of its motive power and coaching stock. One of the stranger facts is that one of its locomotives was used by contractors to lift the lines that it later had to relay. One of the engines on the line was former North London tank engine 58850. In those days one of British Railways' conditions of sale was that BR livery could not be carried and so it regained a former number, 2650. As such it was hired to the demolition contractors and first used to remove the line to Ardingly and later for the section from Horsted Keynes to East Grinstead. Having reached East Grinstead, it ▶

One of the less well remembered engines of the early preservation scene was J52 0-6-0T 1247 seen here at London Bridge on April 1, 1962. It is at the head of a special organised by the Bluebell Railway. Colour-Rail.com

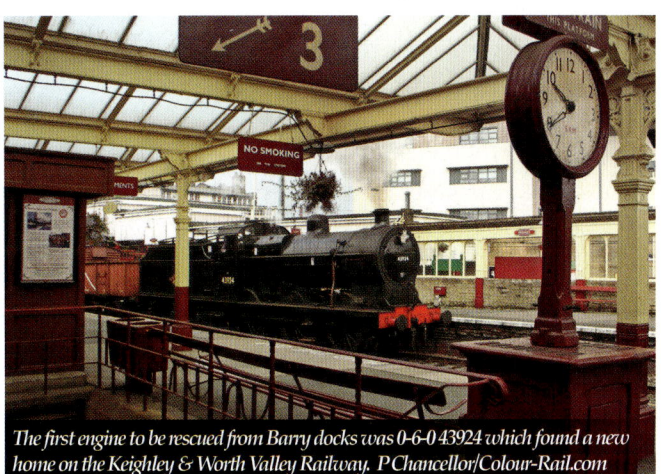

The first engine to be rescued from Barry docks was 0-6-0 43924 which found a new home on the Keighley & Worth Valley Railway. P Chancellor/Colour-Rail.com

Britain's Railways in the 1960s 97

Former North London tank and later BR 58850 found a new home at the Bluebell Railway. It is seen here at Sheffield Park in 1964. It was hired to contractors to help in the lifting of the line from Horsted Keynes to East Grinstead, a length of track later re-laid at great cost by the preservationists. Colour-Rail.com

had to be returned to the Bluebell by road.

Another early starter was the Dart Valley Railway, now known as the South Devon Railway. From the beginning it set out to recreate a GWR branch line and overcame the BR livery ban simply by returning its engines to Great Western guise and painting the coaching stock chocolate and cream with Great Western lettering, so in reality from a distance its trains looked very much like those operating on the main line just a few miles away. Other groups seeking to take over former BR lines included the Keighley & Worth Valley Railway. BR took its time to close the line, so they had a reasonable period to raise the necessary finance. The line was noted in the early years for the bright liveries used on some of its locomotives. It was also one of the first to preserve an item of British Railways modern traction taking in two of the railbuses that had become redundant as early as 1967. Other pioneer organisations were the Kent and East Sussex Railway and what became the North Norfolk Railway.

Back on the narrow gauge, the Welshpool and Llanfair line had been closed by BR and was purchased from them with the track still in situ, unlike the situation encountered by many later railways.

They were also able to buy the two locomotives that had worked the line which had been in store in Oswestry works since closure in 1956. Services restarted in October 1963.

One of the features of early openings was that the 'public' were not allowed to travel on a line until a light railway order was granted. However, trains for members could be run without this requirement being met and so both the Severn Valley Railway and later the North Yorkshire Moors lines operated for some time in this mode, neither opening to the public in the 1960s, although the SVR had accrued a considerable locomotive fleet by the end of the decade. It should be noted that some of the better known heritage lines had not even been on the agenda at the end of the 1960s with the tracks for the likes of the Gloucestershire Warwickshire, Paignton and Dartmouth and the Mid Hants lines still being in daily use by BR.

Finally, mention must be made of the preservation centres that sought to preserve BR infrastructure other than a branch line. The three major centres that evolved in the 1960s were at Didcot for the Great Western Society, Carnforth and Tyseley. At Didcot, the aim was to in due course recreate a Great Western shed environment, whilst Carnforth and Tyseley were more about an operational base. Carnforth was originally intended to house engines to work on what became the Lakeside and Haverthwaite Railway, as at the time through running was possible from Carnforth. However, the line was breached for a new road so the engines for the Lakeside project then transferred to Haverthwaite. Tyseley held open days for enthusiasts and such was its popularity that some 20,000 people attended on September 29, 1968, just six weeks after the end of BR steam.

These were just some of the places where today's vast heritage movement began - the roots of a new industry.

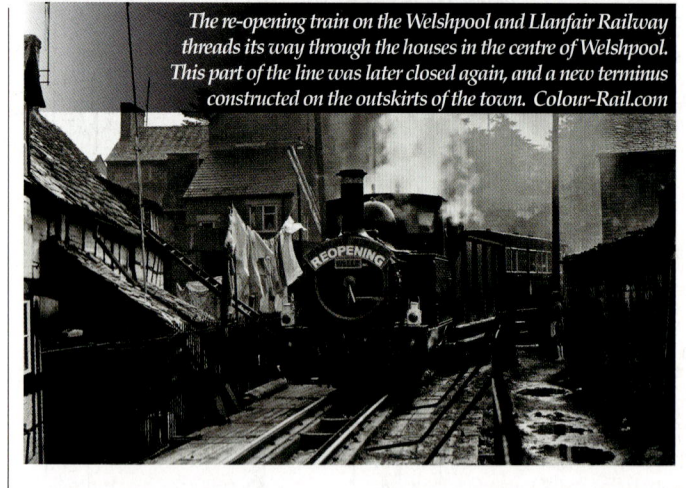

The re-opening train on the Welshpool and Llanfair Railway threads its way through the houses in the centre of Welshpool. This part of the line was later closed again, and a new terminus constructed on the outskirts of the town. Colour-Rail.com

Tyseley's first open day since the ending of BR steam attracted large crowds as seen here - enough to give a modern Health & Safety expert a heart attack. Colour-Rail.com

98

Britain's Railways in the 1960s